SMART SPENDING HANDBOOK:

Practical Household Finance Savvy Tips.

RANDIKA ATTANAYAKA

CONTENTS

To the pillars of my life,

This handbook, "Smart Spending Handbook: Practical Household Finance Savvy Tips," is dedicated with immense gratitude and love to the extraordinary individuals who have shaped my journey.
To my woman, your unwavering support and shared dreams have been my inspiration. This book is a testament to the strength of our partnership and the belief that together, we can navigate the complexities of household finances with savvy and purpose.
To my teachers, your guidance has been invaluable. You've not only imparted knowledge but instilled in me the curiosity to learn and the wisdom to apply that knowledge practically. This book is a reflection of the lessons learned under your tutelage.
To my parents, your unwavering love and sacrifices have laid the foundation for everything I've achieved. This book is a tribute to your resilience, teaching me the value of hard work, responsibility, and the importance of financial literacy.
May the pages of this handbook serve as a small token of my appreciation and a resource to empower others on their financial journeys.
With heartfelt thanks,

Randika Attanayaka (Roo)

CHAPTER 1.

A CREATIVE GUIDE TO TRANSFORMING HOUSEHOLD EXPENSES INTO SAVINGS

I n the complex web of contemporary living, effective management of household expenses is not just a practical necessity but a fundamental step toward ensuring financial stability. This comprehensive guide is designed to illuminate straightforward yet powerful strategies for reducing household costs without necessitating a compromise in one's lifestyle. By assimilating and implementing these strategies, individuals can not only achieve tangible and significant savings but also fortify the foundations for a more secure and resilient financial future.

1. Create A Budget

The foundational cornerstone for any successful financial management plan is the creation of a comprehensive budget. This involves meticulously outlining both your sources of income and monthly expenditures. Categorizing these expenditures offers a granular view of where your money is going, providing the necessary insights to make informed decisions about potential cutbacks and adjustments.

2. Track Your Spending

To truly understand and gain control over your financial landscape, meticulous tracking of daily expenditures is essential. Thanks to modern technology, this task is made more accessible through budgeting apps or digital spreadsheets. This granular tracking not only highlights unnecessary expenses but also empowers individuals to make real-time adjustments to curb frivolous spending habits.

3. Cut Unnecessary Subscriptions

In the era of digital content and convenience services, subscription expenses can quickly accumulate. Take the time to evaluate the necessity of each subscription, whether it be streaming services, magazine subscriptions, or gym memberships. Identifying and subsequently canceling or downgrading services that are not integral to your daily life can result in substantial monthly savings without compromising overall lifestyle quality.

4. Shop Smarter

Transforming grocery shopping into a strategic and planned activity can significantly impact your monthly expenses. By planning meals in advance, creating detailed shopping lists, and sticking to them, individuals can avoid impulse purchases and unnecessary expenditures. Additionally, taking advantage of discounts, loyalty programs, and opting for generic brands can further contribute to financial savings.

5. Energy-Efficient Practices

Reducing utility bills through energy-efficient practices is not just environmentally responsible but also financially savvy. Simple habits such as turning off lights and appliances when not in use, adopting energy-efficient light bulbs, and investing in smart home devices can collectively contribute to noticeable long-term savings on your utility bills.

6. Refinance Debt

For individuals burdened by outstanding loans or credit card debt, exploring opportunities for debt refinancing can be a game-changer. By securing lower interest rates through refinancing, monthly payments can be substantially reduced, providing a tangible and immediate financial reprieve.

7. Diy Projects

Embracing a do-it-yourself mentality for basic household tasks extends beyond just a practical skill; it's a potent financial strategy. Developing basic repair and maintenance skills allows individuals to handle minor household issues without the need for professional services, translating into tangible and recurring savings over time.

8. Review Insurance Policies

A periodic review of insurance policies is essential to ensure optimal coverage at competitive rates. Obtaining quotes from various providers and considering bundling policies can uncover potential discounts, optimizing your insurance-related expenditures without compromising on coverage.

9. Explore Alternative Transportation

In the realm of commuting expenses, exploring alternative transportation options can yield substantial savings. Whether it's opting for public transportation, carpooling with colleagues, biking, or walking, these alternatives not only contribute to a healthier lifestyle but also reduce fuel and maintenance costs associated with personal vehicle ownership.

10. Financial Education

Investing time in enhancing financial literacy is akin to empowering oneself with a formidable tool for long-term financial success. Understanding the fundamentals of investing, exploring different types of savings accounts, and adopting strategic approaches to wealth growth ensures not just effective decision-making but also fosters a proactive and informed financial mindset.

As individuals integrate these practical and actionable strategies

into their daily lives, a transformation occurs wherein they assume control over their household expenses. Starting with minor adjustments and maintaining consistency, these strategies pave the way for the cultivation of a more secure financial foundation, ensuring not just immediate savings but a sustained and resilient financial future.

CHAPTER 2.

THE TOP 7 ADVANTAGES OF ONLINE BANKING: EMBRACE THE FUTURE OF FINANCIAL MANAGEMENT

Discover the numerous advantages of online banking and how it revolutionizes the way we manage our finances. From convenience to enhanced security, explore the top benefits that make online banking a smart choice for individuals and businesses alike.

In today's digital age, online banking has emerged as a game-changer in the realm of financial management. With the click of a button, you can access your accounts, transfer funds, pay bills, and monitor transactions from the comfort of your home or on the go. In this comprehensive guide, we will delve into

the top seven advantages of online banking and explore why it has become an indispensable tool for individuals and businesses worldwide. From convenience and time-saving benefits to enhanced security measures, we will uncover the reasons why online banking has gained such popularity. Whether you're a tech-savvy individual looking to simplify your financial tasks or a business owner seeking efficient cash management solutions, this article will showcase the transformative power of online banking and how it can revolutionize the way you manage your finances.

Advantage 1: Convenience And Accessibility:

Online banking eliminates the need for physical visits to a bank branch. With 24/7 access to your accounts through a secure online portal or mobile app, you can conveniently perform banking transactions anytime, anywhere. This section will highlight the convenience of managing your finances remotely and the flexibility it provides to fit banking tasks into your busy schedule.

Advantage 2: Time-Saving Efficiency:

Say goodbye to long queues and waiting times. Online banking streamlines financial tasks, enabling you to complete them quickly and efficiently. This section will discuss time-saving features such as online bill payments, fund transfers, and the ability to review transactions and account balances in real-time.

Advantage 3: Enhanced Security Measures:

Online banking has evolved with robust security measures to protect your sensitive financial information. We'll explore the advanced encryption technologies, multi-factor authentication, and fraud detection systems employed by banks to ensure the security of your online transactions. This section will emphasize the peace of mind that comes with secure online banking.

Advantage 4: Paperless Environment:

Online banking reduces the need for paper-based statements, receipts, and checks. By opting for electronic statements and online payments, you contribute to a more eco-friendly and sustainable banking experience. We'll discuss the environmental benefits of going paperless and how it aligns with modern-day digital practices.

Advantage 5: Comprehensive Account Management:

Online banking provides a holistic view of your financial accounts in one centralized location. This section will highlight the convenience of monitoring multiple accounts, including checking, savings, credit cards, and loans, from a single online platform. We'll explore features like transaction history, account statements, and the ability to set up customized alerts and notifications.

Advantage 6: Access To Financial Tools And Insights:

Many online banking platforms offer an array of financial tools and insights to help you make informed decisions. This section will explore features such as budgeting tools, spending analysis, and personalized recommendations that empower you to manage your finances effectively and achieve your financial goals.

Advantage 7: Seamless Integration With Other Financial Services:

Online banking seamlessly integrates with various financial services, further enhancing its value. We'll discuss features like online loan applications, investment account access, and the ability to link external accounts for a comprehensive financial ecosystem. This section will highlight the convenience of having all your financial needs in one place.

Online banking has revolutionized the way we manage our finances, offering a wide range of advantages that simplify and enhance the banking experience. From the convenience of 24/7 accessibility and time-saving efficiency to the advanced security measures and comprehensive account management, online banking empowers individuals and businesses alike. Embrace the future of financial management by leveraging the benefits of online banking, and take control of your finances with ease, convenience, and peace of mind. Start enjoying the transformative advantages of online banking today.

Online banking has revolutionized the way we manage our finances, offering a wide range of advantages that simplify and enhance the banking experience. With the convenience of 24/7 accessibility, you no longer need to adjust your schedule to visit a physical bank branch during limited banking hours. Online banking allows you to perform various financial transactions at your convenience, whether it's transferring funds between accounts, paying bills, or managing investments.

One of the significant advantages of online banking is the time-saving efficiency it offers. Long gone are the days of waiting in long queues or dealing with cumbersome paperwork. With online banking, you can complete transactions and access information within minutes. It streamlines financial tasks, allowing you to focus on other aspects of your life.

Security is a top concern when it comes to managing finances, and online banking addresses this with enhanced security measures. Banks employ robust encryption technologies, multi-factor authentication, and real-time fraud detection systems to safeguard your sensitive information. Online banking provides a secure environment for your transactions, giving you peace of mind.

By embracing online banking, you contribute to a paperless environment. Electronic statements, online bill payments, and digital receipts reduce paper waste and have a positive impact on the environment. Going paperless is not only convenient but also aligns with modern-day digital practices.

Online banking offers comprehensive account management by consolidating your financial information in one centralized location. You can view and monitor multiple accounts, including checking, savings, credit cards, and loans, with ease. Having a holistic view of your financial status enables better financial planning and decision-making.

Furthermore, online banking platforms often provide a range of financial tools and insights. Budgeting tools, spending analysis, and personalized recommendations help you understand your financial habits and make informed decisions. You can set financial goals, track your progress, and optimize your financial health.

Seamless integration with other financial services is another advantage of online banking. You can apply for loans, access investment accounts, and link external accounts for a comprehensive financial ecosystem. This integration simplifies financial management and allows for a more cohesive and streamlined experience.

In conclusion, online banking offers a plethora of advantages that revolutionize the way we manage our finances. Its convenience, time-saving efficiency, enhanced security measures, paperless environment, comprehensive account management, access to financial tools and insights, and seamless integration with other financial services make it an essential tool for individuals and businesses alike. Embrace the future of financial management by leveraging the benefits of online banking, and take control of your finances with ease, convenience, and peace of mind. Start enjoying the transformative advantages of online banking today.

CHAPTER 3

INVESTING WISELY IN PERSONAL GROWTH, EDUCATION AND SKILL DEVELOPMENT:

I n the dynamic landscape of today's world, where adaptability and continuous learning are paramount, the pursuit of education and skill development is a strategic investment in personal growth. The exciting aspect is that this investment need not carry a hefty financial burden; there are practical and budget-friendly approaches to enriching your knowledge and skills.

The digital era has revolutionized learning, making it more accessible than ever. Online platforms like Coursera, Udemy, and Khan Academy offer a plethora of courses at affordable prices, and often for free. Whether you're delving into technical skills or exploring the arts and humanities, these platforms provide a flexible and cost-effective gateway to personal development.

In addition to formal online courses, the abundance of free educational resources is staggering. E-books, audiobooks, online tutorials, and educational podcasts offer a wealth of knowledge that is easily accessible. Public libraries further contribute to this culture of accessible learning, providing a treasure trove of educational materials for all.

Community colleges stand out as affordable hubs for education. They offer diverse courses at a fraction of the cost of traditional universities, making education accessible to a broader audience. Continuing education programs within these institutions provide avenues for acquiring new skills without committing to a prolonged degree.

Local workshops and seminars provide immersive learning experiences at minimal costs. Hosted by community organizations and businesses, these events offer hands-on education and networking opportunities. Keeping an eye on local listings and digital platforms ensures you stay informed about upcoming educational opportunities in your area.

Beyond formal education, mentorship and networking are pivotal in personal growth. Connecting with experienced professionals in your field provides invaluable insights and perspectives. Attend networking events, join online communities, and seek mentorship to gain not only knowledge but also real-world advice.

Government programs and scholarships play a crucial role in making education accessible. Exploring scholarship opportunities aligned with your goals and investigating government initiatives supporting skill development can open doors to affordable learning options.

For those currently employed, many employers offer training programs as part of their commitment to professional development. Workshops, webinars, and in-house training sessions can enhance your skills at no additional cost, aligning your personal growth with the goals of your organization.

In essence, the journey of education and skill development is an investment in yourself that need not strain your finances. By strategically navigating the wealth of affordable resources and opportunities available, you are not only enriching your knowledge but also positioning yourself for success in the ever-evolving landscape of personal and professional growth.

1. Embrace Online Learning Platforms:

The digital age has brought forth a wealth of online learning platforms offering courses on a myriad of subjects. Websites like Coursera, Udemy, and Khan Academy provide affordable or even free courses. Whether you're looking to pick up a new language, delve into coding, or enhance your business skills, these platforms offer a cost-effective gateway to education.

2. Explore Free Resources:

Libraries and the internet abound with free resources. From e-books and audiobooks to online tutorials and educational podcasts, there's a treasure trove of knowledge waiting to be explored. Public libraries often offer free access to a wide range of educational materials, making learning accessible to all.

3. Community College And Continuing Education

Programs:

Community colleges are valuable hubs for affordable education. They offer a range of courses at a fraction of the cost of traditional universities. Additionally, many community colleges provide continuing education programs, allowing you to acquire new skills without committing to a lengthy degree.

4. Attend Workshops And Seminars:

Local workshops, seminars, and conferences are excellent opportunities to gain knowledge and network. Many community organizations and businesses host these events, often at low or no cost. Keep an eye on local listings and social media for announcements about upcoming educational events in your area.

5. Seek Mentorship And Networking:

Connecting with experienced professionals in your field of interest can be an invaluable source of education. Seek mentorship opportunities, attend networking events, and join online communities related to your industry. The insights and advice gained from experienced individuals can be as enriching as a formal education.

6. Utilize Government Programs And Scholarships:

Government programs and scholarships are designed to make education accessible to a wide audience. Explore scholarship opportunities that align with your goals and check for government initiatives supporting skill development. These programs often aim to bridge gaps in access to education and training.

7. Leverage Employer Training Programs:

If you're currently employed, inquire about training programs offered by your employer. Many companies invest in the professional development of their employees. Whether it's workshops, webinars, or in-house training, these opportunities can enhance your skills without additional financial strain.

In conclusion, education and skill development need not be a financial burden. By strategically leveraging affordable and free resources, you can invest wisely in your personal growth. Remember, the pursuit of knowledge is a lifelong journey, and every small step you take contributes to your ongoing development and adaptability in a rapidly changing world.

CHAPTER 4.

THE ULTIMATE GUIDE TO CHOOSING THE RIGHT BANK AND MINIMIZING FEES

C hoosing the right bank is a critical financial decision that can significantly impact your savings and financial well-being. This comprehensive guide will provide you with expert advice on selecting the perfect bank to meet your needs while also helping you avoid unnecessary fees. By following the strategies outlined in this article, you'll gain the knowledge and insights necessary to make an informed decision, ensuring that your hard-earned money is safeguarded and maximizing your financial benefits.

When it comes to managing our finances, choosing the right bank is a crucial decision. Not all banks are created equal, and finding one that suits your needs can save you from unnecessary fees and charges. In this comprehensive guide, we will walk you through the essential factors to consider when selecting a bank and provide practical tips to avoid expensive fees. By the end of this article, you'll be equipped with the knowledge to make an informed decision and ensure your financial well-being.

Assess Your Banking Needs, Conduct Thorough Research, Compare Account Fees and Policies, Evaluate Convenience and Technology, Consider Customer Service and Support, Seek Recommendations and Read Reviews, Understand the Importance of Security, Don't Overlook Credit Unions and Online Banks, Utilize Bank Account Switching Services, Regularly Review and Optimize Your Bank Accounts, Assess Your Banking Needs: Before you start exploring different bank options, take a moment to assess your banking needs. Consider your financial goals, transaction patterns, and the specific services you require. Are you looking for a basic checking account for day-to-day transactions, a high-yield savings account to grow your savings, or specialized services like mortgages or investment accounts? Understanding your needs will help you narrow down your options and find a bank that offers the services you require.

Conduct Thorough Research:

Research is key when it comes to finding the right bank. Look for reputable financial institutions that have a solid track record and positive customer reviews. Check if the bank is insured by the Federal Deposit Insurance Corporation (FDIC) or the National Credit Union Administration (NCUA) for added protection. Explore their websites to learn about the account types they offer, fees associated with each account, interest rates, and any special promotions or benefits.

Compare Account Fees And Policies:

One of the primary reasons people end up paying excessive fees is a lack of awareness about the fee structures of their chosen bank. Carefully examine the fee schedules provided by potential banks. Pay attention to monthly maintenance fees, ATM withdrawal charges, overdraft fees, and penalties for low balances. Look for banks that offer fee waivers or reduced fees based on specific criteria, such as maintaining a minimum balance or setting up direct deposits.

Evaluate Convenience And Technology:

Consider the convenience and accessibility factors offered by different banks. Evaluate their branch and ATM network coverage to ensure you can easily access your funds when needed. Determine whether they offer online and mobile banking services, as well as features like mobile check deposit, bill payment, and budgeting tools. The availability of 24/7 customer support and robust security measures should also be considered.

Consider Customer Service And Support:

Good customer service and support are essential for a positive banking experience. Look for banks that have a reputation for providing excellent customer service. Consider factors such as responsiveness, availability of live chat or phone support, and the bank's commitment to resolving customer issues promptly. A bank that values customer satisfaction will ensure that your concerns are addressed effectively.

Seek Recommendations And Read Reviews:

Don't hesitate to seek recommendations from friends, family, or colleagues who have had positive experiences with their banks. Additionally, read online reviews and forums to gather insights from other customers. While individual experiences may vary, a general consensus can provide valuable information about a bank's customer service, fees, and overall satisfaction levels.

Understand The Importance Of Security:

Security should be a top priority when choosing a bank. Look for banks that employ advanced security measures such as encryption, multi-factor authentication, and fraud detection systems. Check if the bank has a solid reputation for safeguarding customer information and promptly addressing security breaches. Your peace of mind and the protection of your financial data should not be compromised.

Don't Overlook Credit Unions And Online Banks:

While traditional banks may come to mind first, credit unions and online banks can offer compelling alternatives. Credit unions are not-for-profit financial cooperatives that often provide competitive rates and lower fees. Online banks, with their lower overhead costs, can offer higher interest rates and reduced fees. Don't overlook these options during your search for the right bank.

Utilize Bank Account Switching Services: If you're dissatisfied with your current bank and want to switch, take advantage of bank account switching services. Some banks offer assistance in transferring your accounts, automatic bill payments, and direct deposits from your previous bank. Utilizing these services can simplify the process and ensure a smooth transition to your new bank.

Regularly Review And Optimize Your Bank Accounts:

Choosing the right bank is not a one-time decision. It's important to regularly review your bank accounts to ensure they continue to meet your needs and offer competitive terms. Stay updated on any changes in fees, policies, or services that may impact your banking experience. If you find that your current bank no longer meets your requirements, be proactive in exploring other options.

Choosing the right bank and minimizing fees requires careful consideration and thorough research. By assessing your needs, conducting thorough research, comparing account fees and policies, evaluating convenience and technology, considering customer service and support, seeking recommendations, understanding security measures, exploring credit unions and online banks, utilizing bank account switching services, and regularly reviewing and optimizing your bank accounts, you can make an informed decision that aligns with your financial goals. Remember, a well-chosen bank can provide a solid foundation for your financial success and help you avoid unnecessary expenses.

By assessing your banking needs, conducting thorough research, comparing fees and policies, evaluating convenience and technology, and seeking recommendations, you can make an informed decision that minimizes fees and maximizes your financial benefits. Remember, a diligent selection process will lead to a long-lasting banking relationship that aligns with your goals and supports your financial well-being.

"Do not save what is left after spending, but spend what is left after saving."

Warren Buffett

CHAPTER 5.

6 SMART STRATEGIES FOR PLANNING YOUR HOUSEHOLD BUDGET ON A LIMITED INCOME

Managing your household budget on a limited income can be a challenging endeavor, but with careful planning and smart strategies, it is possible to achieve financial stability and make the most of your resources. Whether you are facing financial constraints due to a lower income, unexpected expenses, or simply want to optimize your budget, this comprehensive guide will provide you with practical insights and effective techniques to plan your household budget effectively.

In today's fast-paced and ever-changing world, financial planning is essential for individuals and families alike. It serves as a roadmap to ensure that your income is allocated wisely, expenses are managed effectively, and financial goals are pursued with determination. Planning your household budget becomes even more crucial when you are working with a limited income, as it requires careful consideration of your financial priorities and strategic decision-making.

Throughout this guide, we will explore various strategies and principles that can help you navigate the process of budget planning on a limited income. We will delve into assessing your financial situation, setting realistic goals, creating a comprehensive budget, maximizing your income, and making wise choices when it comes to expenses. By implementing these strategies, you will be equipped with the knowledge and tools to make informed financial decisions and create a solid foundation for your financial future.

It's important to note that budget planning is not a one-size-fits-all approach. Each individual or family has unique circumstances and financial goals. The strategies and techniques outlined in this guide are meant to serve as a framework from which you can tailor your own budgeting plan that aligns with your specific needs and aspirations.

It's also worth mentioning that budgeting is not about depriving yourself or living a restricted lifestyle. Instead, it is about making conscious choices and prioritizing your financial well-being. With the right mindset and a proactive approach, you can effectively manage your limited income, minimize financial stress, and work towards achieving your financial goals.

So, if you're ready to take control of your finances and make the most of your limited income, let's dive into the smart strategies for planning your household budget.

1. Assessing Your Financial Situation:

Before you start budget planning, it's essential to have a clear understanding of your current financial situation. Begin by evaluating your income sources, which may include your salary, freelance work, or any other side gigs. Be sure to calculate your income after taxes to have an accurate figure for budgeting. Next, track your expenses for a month or two to identify where your money is going. Categorize your spending into essentials (such as housing, utilities, groceries) and discretionary items (like dining out, entertainment). This exercise will help you spot areas where you can potentially cut costs.

2. Setting Realistic Financial Goals:

Establishing clear and achievable financial goals is crucial to staying motivated and focused. Identify both short-term and long-term objectives, such as building an emergency fund, paying off debts, saving for a down payment, or investing for retirement. Prioritize your goals based on urgency and importance. Ensure that your goals are specific, measurable, attainable, relevant, and time-bound (SMART). For instance, if you want to save for a vacation, determine the exact amount needed and set a timeframe to reach that target.

3. Creating A Comprehensive Budget:

A well-structured budget is the foundation of successful financial planning. Start by categorizing your expenses into fixed (unchanging) and variable (fluctuating) costs. Fixed expenses may include rent/mortgage, insurance premiums, and loan payments, while variable expenses can include groceries, transportation, and entertainment. Allocate funds for each category based on your income and priorities. Aim to save at least 20% of your income, if possible, for both short-term and long-term goals. Consider using budgeting apps or spreadsheets to track your spending and stay on top of your financial plan.

4. Maximizing Your Income:

When dealing with a limited income, finding ways to increase your earnings can make a significant difference. Consider taking up a side hustle or freelance work in your spare time to supplement your primary income. Leverage your skills and talents to offer services or products that align with your interests. Negotiating a raise or exploring opportunities for career advancement within your current job can also lead to increased income. Additionally, consider passive income streams, such as investing in stocks, real estate, or creating digital products that generate revenue over time.

5. Cutting Expenses Wisely:

Reducing unnecessary expenses is a vital aspect of budget planning. Begin by analyzing your discretionary spending and identifying areas where you can cut back. Look for subscription services you no longer use or negotiate better rates for bills like cable or internet. Practice frugal living by opting for homemade meals instead of dining out frequently, finding free or low-cost entertainment options, and buying items on sale or second-hand when possible. Small adjustments in your daily habits can lead to significant savings in the long run.

6. Managing Debt Strategically:

If you have outstanding debts, managing them efficiently is essential to stay on track with your budget. Prioritize paying off high-interest debts first while making minimum payments on others. Consider debt consolidation to streamline multiple payments into a single, manageable one. If you're struggling to meet debt obligations, communicate with creditors to negotiate more favorable terms or explore hardship programs. Seeking professional advice from credit counseling agencies can also provide valuable guidance for debt management.

Creating a household budget and managing your finances on a limited income requires discipline, patience, and smart decision-making. By assessing your financial situation, setting realistic goals, creating a comprehensive budget, maximizing your income, and cutting expenses wisely, you can take control of your financial future.

Remember, financial planning is a continuous process that requires regular review and adjustments. Stay committed to your budget, track your progress, and celebrate milestones along the way. With dedication and perseverance, you can achieve financial stability, reduce stress, and build a better future for yourself and your family, regardless of your income limitations.

Always consult with financial professionals for personalized advice based on your specific circumstances.

CHAPTER 6.

BUDGETING BLUNDERS: 6 COMMON MISTAKES YOU MUST AVOID FOR FINANCIAL SUCCESS

C reating a budget is a fundamental step towards financial stability and achieving your long-term goals. It helps you take control of your finances, manage your income and expenses effectively, and make informed financial decisions. However, even with the best intentions, many individuals unknowingly fall into common budgeting mistakes that can have detrimental effects on their financial health. In this blog post, we will delve into the six most common budget mistakes that you simply cannot afford to make. By understanding and avoiding these pitfalls, you can maximize the effectiveness of your budget and pave the way for a more secure financial future.

When it comes to budgeting, knowledge is power. The more aware you are of the potential mistakes and challenges that lie ahead, the better equipped you'll be to overcome them. By addressing these common budgeting mistakes head-on, you can stay on track, maintain financial discipline, and avoid unnecessary setbacks.

In this comprehensive guide, we will explore each budgeting mistake in detail and provide practical tips and strategies to overcome them. From underestimating expenses and neglecting emergency funds to overlooking debt repayment and failing to plan for irregular expenses, we will tackle these issues one by one. By identifying these pitfalls and implementing effective solutions, you'll be well on your way to a stronger and more successful budgeting journey.

Budgeting is not about restricting your financial freedom or depriving yourself of the things you enjoy. On the contrary, it is a powerful tool that empowers you to align your spending with your financial goals and priorities. By avoiding these common budget mistakes, you can ensure that your hard-earned money is allocated wisely and that you are making progress towards your desired financial outcomes.

It's important to remember that budgeting is a dynamic process. It requires regular evaluation, adjustments, and a willingness to learn from your financial experiences. As you navigate the world of budgeting, keep an open mind and be prepared to make changes as necessary. By continuously refining your budget and staying proactive, you'll be able to adapt to shifting circumstances and optimize your financial well-being.

In the following sections, we will delve into each of the six common budget mistakes in detail, providing practical insights and actionable tips to help you avoid them. By the end of this guide, you'll be equipped with the knowledge and tools to create a more effective budget, overcome obstacles, and pave the way for a more secure and prosperous financial future.

1. Underestimating Expenses:

One of the most common mistakes people make when budgeting is underestimating their expenses. It's crucial to have a realistic understanding of your monthly bills, including utilities, rent or mortgage payments, insurance, and transportation costs. Neglecting to account for these essential expenses can lead to overspending and financial stress. Take the time to track your expenses accurately and adjust your budget accordingly.

2. Neglecting Emergency Funds:

Failing to prioritize an emergency fund is a critical budgeting mistake. Life is unpredictable, and unexpected expenses can quickly derail your financial plans. Aim to set aside a portion of your income each month to build an emergency fund that covers three to six months' worth of living expenses. Having this safety net will provide peace of mind and protect you from accumulating debt in times of crisis.

3. Ignoring Debt Repayment:

Ignoring debt repayment is a significant setback for your financial health. Many individuals make the mistake of neglecting their debts or only making minimum payments. This approach prolongs the repayment process and results in accumulating interest charges. Prioritize debt repayment in your budget and allocate extra funds towards paying off debts systematically. Consider using the debt snowball or debt avalanche method to accelerate your progress.

4. Failing To Plan For Irregular Expenses:

Irregular expenses, such as annual subscriptions, car maintenance, or holiday expenses, are often overlooked in budgeting. Failing to plan for these costs can lead to financial strain when they arise unexpectedly. Identify your irregular expenses, estimate their annual cost, and divide that amount by twelve to determine the monthly contribution required. By including these expenses in your budget, you can avoid last-minute financial surprises.

5. Overlooking Small Purchases:

Small, seemingly insignificant purchases can add up quickly and derail your budget. Coffee shop visits, impulse buys, or frequent dining out can significantly impact your financial stability. Practice mindful spending and track your expenses diligently. Consider adopting the "30-day rule" for non-essential purchases, giving yourself time to assess if you truly need or want an item before buying it.

6. Failing To Review And Adjust:

A budget is not a one-time creation but an evolving tool that requires regular review and adjustment. Failing to reassess your budget periodically can lead to outdated or unrealistic financial plans. Set aside time each month to review your income, expenses, and progress towards your financial goals. Make necessary adjustments to ensure your budget reflects your current financial situation and priorities.

Avoiding common budgeting mistakes is essential for achieving financial stability and ensuring that your hard-earned money is utilized effectively. By recognizing and addressing the six common budget mistakes highlighted in this guide – underestimating expenses, neglecting emergency funds, ignoring debt repayment, failing to plan for irregular expenses, overlooking small purchases, and neglecting budget review – you can significantly improve your financial situation and work towards your long-term goals.

Budgeting is a dynamic process that requires ongoing attention and adjustments. It's crucial to review your budget regularly, track your progress, and make necessary modifications as your financial circumstances change. By staying proactive and staying accountable to your budget, you'll be able to maintain financial discipline and make informed financial decisions.

Remember, budgeting is not about depriving yourself of enjoyment or living a restricted lifestyle. It's about finding a balance between your financial priorities and your personal values. By making conscious choices and aligning your spending with your goals, you can live a fulfilling life while still achieving financial success.

Incorporating smart strategies into your budgeting process, such as accurately estimating your expenses, prioritizing emergency funds, tackling debt systematically, planning for irregular expenses, being mindful of small purchases, and regularly reviewing and adjusting your budget, will set you on the path towards financial empowerment.

As you embark on your budgeting journey, remember that it's a marathon, not a sprint. Be patient with yourself, stay committed to your financial goals, and celebrate small victories along the way. By avoiding these common budgeting mistakes and developing healthy financial habits, you can build a solid foundation for a secure and prosperous future.

Always keep in mind that financial success is a journey unique to each individual. Seek personalized advice from financial professionals if needed, as they can provide guidance tailored to your specific circumstances and goals. With determination, discipline, and the knowledge gained from this guide, you can overcome budgeting pitfalls and create a brighter financial future for yourself.

CHAPTER 7.

MASTER YOUR FINANCES: DISCOVER THE 7 BEST FREE BUDGETING APPS FOR EFFECTIVE MONEY MANAGEMENT

In today's fast-paced world, managing personal finances can often feel like a daunting task. From tracking expenses to setting financial goals, it's crucial to have effective money management strategies in place. Thankfully, with the rise of technology, budgeting apps have emerged as powerful tools to help individuals gain control over their finances. These apps offer features that simplify the budgeting process, provide valuable insights, and empower users to make informed financial decisions.

In this article, we will explore the world of budgeting apps and present you with the 7 best free options available. These apps have been carefully selected based on their features, user-friendliness, and positive user reviews. Whether you're a seasoned budgeter or just starting to take charge of your financial journey, these apps will serve as your trusted companions, helping you master your finances and achieve your financial goals.

Financial management is a crucial aspect of our lives. By having a clear understanding of our income, expenses, and financial goals, we can make smarter choices that pave the way for a secure financial future. The beauty of budgeting apps lies in their ability to streamline the process, making it easier and more convenient for users to track their spending, set budgets, and analyze their financial patterns.

With the wide array of budgeting apps available, it's essential to choose the one that aligns with your specific needs and preferences. The apps featured in this guide offer a diverse range of features and approaches, ensuring that there's something for everyone. Whether you're seeking comprehensive financial tracking, goal-setting capabilities, or simplified expense management, you'll find an app that suits your unique requirements.

In the following sections, we will delve into each of the 7 best free budgeting apps, exploring their standout features, benefits, and user experiences. We'll discuss how these apps can help you gain control over your finances, improve your spending habits, and work towards your financial aspirations. By the end of this guide, you'll have a clear understanding of the top budgeting apps available, enabling you to make an informed decision and embark on a path towards financial success.

It's important to note that while these budgeting apps can be powerful tools, they are not magic solutions. Successful money management requires discipline, commitment, and an ongoing effort to stay actively engaged with your financial situation. The apps we'll discuss are meant to complement your efforts, provide guidance, and simplify the process, but ultimately, it's up to you to take ownership of your financial well-being.

1. Mint:

Mint is a popular and feature-rich budgeting app that allows you to connect your bank accounts, credit cards, and other financial accounts in one place. It automatically categorizes your transactions, provides budgeting tools, and sends alerts for bill payments and upcoming expenses. With its intuitive interface and comprehensive financial overview, Mint is an excellent choice for individuals seeking a free and all-in-one budgeting solution.

The official website of Mint is:
www.mint.com

2. Personal Capital:

Personal Capital combines budgeting and investment tracking into one powerful platform. It offers tools to manage your budget, track your net worth, and analyze your investment portfolio. With Personal Capital, you can gain a holistic view of your financial situation and make informed decisions for long-term financial success.

The official website of Personal Capital is:
www.personalcapital.com

3. Ynab (You Need A Budget):

YNAB follows a unique "zero-based" budgeting approach, where every dollar is assigned a specific purpose. It helps you prioritize your spending, set realistic goals, and break the cycle of living paycheck to paycheck. YNAB's proactive budgeting philosophy and user-friendly interface make it a valuable tool for those looking to take control of their finances.

The official website of YNAB (You Need a Budget) is:
www.youneedabudget.com

4. Pocketguard:

PocketGuard simplifies budgeting by providing a clear snapshot of your financial picture. It tracks your income, expenses, and savings goals, ensuring you stay within your budget. PocketGuard also offers smart spending notifications and provides insights into how you can save more and optimize your expenses.

The official website of PocketGuard is:
www.pocketguard.com

5. Wally:

Wally is a straightforward budgeting app designed to help you track expenses and set savings goals. With its intuitive interface and expense categorization features, Wally allows you to visualize your spending patterns and make more informed financial decisions. It also offers features like receipt scanning and foreign currency tracking, making it an ideal choice for those who want a simple yet effective budgeting tool.

The official website of Wally is:
www.wally.me

6. Goodbudget:

Goodbudget follows the envelope budgeting system, where you

allocate funds to different categories or "envelopes." It provides a digital version of this system, allowing you to set spending limits and track your progress. Goodbudget is particularly beneficial for individuals who prefer a visual representation of their budget and want to practice mindful spending.

The official website of Goodbudget is: www.goodbudget.com/

7. Clarity Money:

Clarity Money aims to simplify your financial life by helping you track expenses, find ways to save, and manage subscriptions. It provides insights into your spending habits and offers personalized suggestions to optimize your finances. Clarity Money's subscription management feature is especially useful for keeping track of recurring expenses.

The official website of Clarity Money is: www.claritymoney.com

Effective money management is crucial for achieving financial stability and realizing your financial goals. The 7 best free budgeting apps we've explored in this guide offer a range of features and functionalities to assist you in mastering your finances. These apps can simplify the budgeting process, provide valuable insights into your spending habits, and empower you to make informed financial decisions.

While each app has its unique strengths and focus areas, they all share the common goal of helping you take control of your financial situation. Whether you're looking for comprehensive expense tracking, goal-setting capabilities, or simplified budget management, there's an app that suits your specific needs and preferences.

However, it's important to remember that a budgeting app alone is not a cure-all solution. To truly master your finances, you need to actively engage with the app, regularly review your budget, and make adjustments as needed. These apps serve as valuable tools to guide and support your financial journey, but ultimately, your commitment and discipline are key to achieving long-term financial success.

As you explore the various budgeting apps, consider your financial goals, preferences, and comfort level with technology. Experiment with different apps to find the one that resonates with you and integrates seamlessly into your lifestyle. Remember, what works for one person may not work for another, so it's essential to find an app that suits your unique circumstances.

Additionally, while budgeting apps can provide valuable insights and automate certain aspects of money management, it's still important to stay engaged with your finances. Regularly review your budget, track your spending, and reassess your financial goals. A budgeting app is a tool to assist you in this process, but the ultimate responsibility lies with you.

By leveraging the power of budgeting apps and adopting smart money management practices, you can take control of your financial future. Stay committed, stay disciplined, and make use of the resources available to you. With the right mindset and the support of these top budgeting apps, you can achieve financial freedom, build a strong foundation for your future, and make your financial dreams a reality.

Start your journey towards financial empowerment today and embrace the power of these incredible budgeting apps. Your path to mastering your finances begins now.

CHAPTER 8.

THRIFTY TACTICS: HOW TO STRETCH YOUR BUDGET AND MAXIMIZE SAVINGS DURING FINANCIAL CRUNCH

I n today's challenging economic landscape, many individuals and families face the need to stretch their budgets and make the most of their limited income. Whether you're dealing with unexpected expenses, a reduction in income, or simply aiming to be more financially mindful, mastering the art of budgeting becomes crucial. This blog post will guide you through a comprehensive set of thrifty tactics designed to help you navigate financial crunches and maximize your savings.

When money is tight, it's crucial to adopt smart strategies to stretch your budget and make every dollar count. Financial crunches can happen to anyone, whether due to unexpected expenses, job loss, or other unforeseen circumstances. However, by implementing thrifty tactics and practicing mindful spending, you can navigate through challenging times and maximize your savings.

In this blog post, we will explore practical and effective ways to stretch your budget and make the most of your limited resources. By incorporating these thrifty tactics into your daily life, you can reduce expenses, eliminate unnecessary spending, and build a stronger financial foundation for the future.

With the strategies outlined in this post, you'll learn how to make every dollar count and prioritize your spending effectively. By incorporating these thrifty tactics into your daily life, you'll not only overcome financial challenges but also develop long-lasting habits that will serve you well in the future.

Why is Budget Stretching Important?

Budget stretching goes beyond mere frugality; it involves making informed and intentional decisions about how you allocate your hard-earned money. During times of financial crunch, every dollar counts, and finding ways to optimize your spending becomes essential. By stretching your budget, you can:

Weather Unexpected Financial Storms:

Life is full of surprises, and financial emergencies can occur when you least expect them. By incorporating thrifty tactics into your daily life, you can build a financial safety net that cushions the impact of unexpected expenses.

Reduce Financial Stress:

Living paycheck to paycheck or constantly worrying about money can take a toll on your mental and emotional well-being. Stretching your budget enables you to gain more financial security and peace of mind.

Improve Money Management Skills:

When resources are scarce, it becomes essential to fine-tune your money management skills. Budget stretching challenges you to think creatively, prioritize expenses, and identify areas where you can make cost-effective choices.

Achieve Financial Goals:

Whether you dream of purchasing a home, paying off debt, or building an emergency fund, budget-stretching paves the way for achieving your long-term financial goals. Cultivate a Thrifty Mindset: Adopting thrifty habits not only benefits you during financial crunches but also instils a mindful approach to spending and consumption. You'll find that many of these habits continue to serve you well, even during financially stable periods.

Navigating through this Guide:

In this guide, we've compiled a wealth of information, tips, and actionable strategies to help you thrive during a financial crunch. Here's an overview of what you can expect from each section:

1. Track Your Expenses:

The first step towards stretching your budget is to gain a

clear understanding of where your money is going. Track your expenses diligently, either through a budgeting app or by maintaining a detailed spreadsheet. Categorize your expenses to identify areas where you can cut back and make adjustments. Having a clear picture of your spending habits lets you make informed decisions and prioritize your financial goals.

2. Create A Realistic Budget:

Once you have an overview of your expenses, create a realistic budget that aligns with your income. Focus on essential expenses such as housing, utilities, and groceries, and allocate a portion of your income towards savings or debt repayment. Be mindful of setting achievable goals and avoid overspending in non-essential categories. A well-planned budget will serve as your roadmap to financial stability.

3. Reduce Discretionary Spending:

During a financial crunch, it's crucial to limit discretionary spending. Evaluate your discretionary expenses such as dining out, entertainment, and shopping. Look for opportunities to cut back without sacrificing too much. For example, instead of eating out, try cooking meals at home and exploring affordable entertainment options like free community events or DIY projects. Small adjustments in discretionary spending can add up to significant savings.

4. Prioritize And Negotiate Bills:

When money is tight, it's essential to prioritize your bills. Start by paying essential bills such as rent or mortgage, utilities, and insurance. If you're struggling to meet payments, contact your service providers and explain your situation. Often, they may offer flexible payment options or assistance programs. Negotiate bills such as internet or cable services to secure lower rates. Every dollar saved counts during a financial crunch.

5. Shop Smart:

Stretch your budget further by adopting smart shopping habits. Compare prices, look for discounts, and consider buying in bulk for essential items. Plan your meals in advance and create a shopping list to avoid impulse purchases. Consider shopping at discount stores or using coupons to maximize savings. Additionally, explore thrift stores or online marketplaces for affordable clothing and household items. Being a savvy shopper can significantly impact your budget.

6. Cut Back On Subscriptions:

Review your subscriptions and identify those that you can do without. Evaluate streaming services, gym memberships, or magazine subscriptions that you rarely use. Cancel or temporarily suspend subscriptions that are not essential. Remember, you can always resubscribe when your financial situation improves. Cutting back on subscriptions can free up funds for more necessary expenses.

7. Save On Utilities:

Lowering your utility bills can contribute to significant savings over time. Turn off lights and unplug electronics when not in use, adjust your thermostat to conserve energy, and consider installing energy-efficient appliances. Additionally, explore options to reduce water consumption, such as fixing leaks and using water-saving devices. These minor adjustments can make a noticeable difference in your monthly utility bills.

8. Explore Diy And Repurposing:

Get creative and explore do-it-yourself (DIY) projects or repurposing items instead of buying new ones. DIY projects can range from simple home repairs to crafting homemade gifts. Repurposing items can extend their lifespan and save you money. For example, turn old jars into storage containers or transform worn-out clothing into rags. Embracing a DIY and repurposing mindset can help you save money while fostering your creativity.

Stretching your budget during a financial crunch requires a combination of discipline, planning, and resourcefulness. By implementing thrifty tactics and making mindful spending choices, you can effectively manage your finances and maximize your savings. Remember to track your expenses, create a realistic budget, reduce discretionary spending, prioritize bills, shop smart, cut back on subscriptions, save on utilities, and explore DIY and repurposing options.

Each step you take towards stretching your budget brings you closer to financial stability and peace of mind. Embrace these thrifty tactics and adapt them to your unique circumstances. Over time, you'll develop healthy financial habits that will not only help you navigate through tough times but also set the foundation for long-term financial success. Start implementing these strategies today and take control of your finances.

CHAPTER 9.

BUILDING YOUR FINANCIAL SAFETY NET: A GUIDE TO EFFECTIVELY PUTTING AWAY EMERGENCY FUNDS

Welcome to our comprehensive guide on building your financial safety net and effectively putting away emergency funds. Life is full of unexpected surprises, and having a solid financial cushion can provide you with peace of mind and protect you from unforeseen financial hardships. In this article, we will explore the importance of emergency funds, how to determine the right amount to save, and practical strategies to help you consistently contribute towards this vital financial resource.

In a world of uncertainties, having a solid financial safety net is paramount to weathering the storms of life. Welcome to our comprehensive guide on building your financial safety net and effectively putting away emergency funds. From unexpected medical expenses to sudden car repairs or unforeseen job losses, life is full of surprises that can have a significant impact on your financial well-being. Having a dedicated fund in place can provide you with peace of mind and protect you from falling into debt or relying on high-interest credit cards during challenging times.

In this article, we will explore the importance of emergency funds, how to determine the right amount to save, and practical strategies to help you consistently contribute towards this vital financial resource. By understanding the significance of an emergency fund and implementing smart saving techniques, you can safeguard your financial future and gain the confidence to navigate through unexpected situations with ease.

Why Building an Emergency Fund is Crucial:

Emergencies come unannounced, and being financially prepared can make all the difference. An emergency fund serves as a financial cushion that allows you to tackle unexpected expenses without disrupting your regular budget or dipping into long-term savings. It acts as a safety net during times of financial uncertainty, providing you with a sense of security and stability.

Whether it's a sudden medical emergency, an urgent home repair, or an unexpected job loss, having readily available funds can prevent you from falling into financial distress. Instead of relying on credit cards or loans with high interest rates, you can draw from your emergency fund to cover the costs and avoid accumulating debt.

Determining the Right Amount for Your Emergency Fund:

One of the crucial aspects of building an effective emergency fund is determining the right amount to save. While there is no one-size-fits-all approach, financial experts often recommend setting aside three to six months' worth of living expenses. However, the ideal amount varies based on individual circumstances.

Factors such as your monthly expenses, job stability, the number of dependents, and any existing insurance coverage should be considered. Additionally, your risk tolerance and long-term financial goals play a role in defining the appropriate size of your emergency fund. We will explore these factors in detail to help you assess and set a realistic savings goal tailored to your specific needs.

Strategies to Effectively Build Your Emergency Fund:

1. Set Clear Savings Goals:

Start by setting specific savings goals for your emergency fund. This will help you stay motivated and focused on consistently contributing towards your target amount. Break down your overall goal into smaller milestones to make it more achievable.

2. Create A Budget And Prioritize Savings:

Developing a budget is crucial for managing your finances effectively. Allocate a portion of your income specifically for your emergency fund and make it a priority. Identify areas where you can reduce expenses and redirect those savings towards your fund.

3. Automate Savings:

Take advantage of automation tools provided by your bank

or financial institution. Set up automatic transfers from your paycheck or checking account to your emergency fund. This eliminates the temptation to spend the money elsewhere and ensures consistent contributions over time.

4. Cut Unnecessary Expenses:

Review your expenses and identify non-essential items or services that can be temporarily eliminated or reduced. Redirect the money saved from these cutbacks towards your emergency fund. Remember, every dollar counts when building your financial safety net.

5. Increase Your Income:

Consider exploring additional income streams to boost your savings efforts. This can include freelancing, part-time work, or selling unused items. The extra income generated can be directed towards your emergency fund, accelerating your progress.

6. Save Windfalls And Bonuses:

When unexpected windfalls or bonuses come your way, resist the temptation to splurge. Instead, allocate a portion or the entirety of these unexpected funds towards your emergency fund. This allows you to make significant strides in building your safety net without impacting your regular budget.

7. Review And Adjust Regularly:

Regularly evaluate your progress and reassess your savings goals. Life circumstances may change, requiring you to adjust the target amount or the timeline for achieving your emergency fund goals. Stay flexible and make necessary adjustments to keep your financial plan on track.

The Benefits of an Emergency Fund:

Having a well-funded emergency fund provides numerous benefits beyond financial security. It:

1. Reduces Stress And Anxiety:

Knowing you have a safety net to fall back on in times of crisis alleviates the stress and anxiety associated with unexpected financial burdens.

2. Prevents Debt Accumulation:

With an emergency fund, you can avoid resorting to credit cards or loans to cover unforeseen expenses. This helps you maintain financial stability and avoid accumulating unnecessary debt.

3. Enables Quick Response:

Having readily available funds allows you to respond promptly to emergencies, whether it's medical expenses, home repairs, or a sudden job loss. You can take action without delay and minimize the impact on your overall financial well-being.

4. Provides Peace Of Mind:

Building an emergency fund brings peace of mind, knowing that you are prepared to handle unexpected situations. It gives you a sense of control and confidence in your financial future.

Building a financial safety net through an emergency fund is a crucial step in securing your financial future. By having funds readily available for unexpected expenses, you can protect yourself from falling into debt and mitigate the financial impact of emergencies. Remember, building an emergency fund requires consistent effort, discipline, and a long-term perspective.

Start by understanding the importance of having an emergency fund and determining the right amount to save based on your unique circumstances. Implement practical strategies like setting clear savings goals, creating a budget, automating savings, cutting unnecessary expenses, and increasing your income. Regularly review your progress and make adjustments as needed.

By following these smart saving techniques, you can build a robust financial safety net and gain the peace of mind that comes with being financially prepared for any unexpected challenges that may come your way.

"Beware of little expenses. A small leak will sink a great ship."

Benjamin Franklin

CHAPTER 10.

DON'T OVERLOOK THESE 9 COMMONLY FORGOTTEN EXPENSES IN YOUR HOUSEHOLD BUDGET

Budgeting is an essential tool for effective financial management, helping individuals take control of their income and expenses. However, even the most diligent budgeters often overlook certain expenses that can significantly impact their financial plans. In this article, we will shed light on nine commonly forgotten expenses in household budgets. By being aware of these expenses and proactively including them in your budgeting process, you can achieve greater financial stability and avoid unnecessary stress.

Proper budgeting goes beyond tracking the obvious monthly expenses like rent, groceries, and utilities. It requires a holistic approach that takes into account both the expected and unexpected costs that can arise in various areas of life. By recognizing and planning for commonly forgotten expenses, you can avoid financial surprises and better allocate your resources to meet your financial goals.

As you delve into the details of these commonly overlooked expenses, you'll gain insights into how they can impact your overall budget and financial well-being. Whether you are just starting your budgeting journey or looking to refine your existing budget, understanding and addressing these forgotten expenses is a crucial step towards achieving financial success.

Budgeting is not a one-size-fits-all approach, and everyone's financial situation and priorities may differ. However, by incorporating these often-forgotten expenses into your budgeting process, you can ensure a more accurate representation of your financial reality. This will allow you to make informed decisions, manage your resources effectively, and maintain financial stability in the face of unexpected costs.

In the following sections, we will explore each of these commonly forgotten expenses in detail, providing insights and practical tips on how to incorporate them into your budget. By the end of this article, you'll be equipped with the knowledge and strategies to enhance your budgeting skills and achieve a more comprehensive understanding of your household finances.

Remember, the key to successful budgeting lies in being proactive and adaptable. Regularly review and revise your budget to accommodate changes in your financial situation and priorities. With a well-rounded budget that considers all aspects of your financial obligations, you can navigate the twists and turns of life with greater confidence and financial resilience. Let's dive in and uncover the commonly forgotten expenses that could be impacting your household budget.

1. Home Maintenance And Repairs:

Homeownership comes with various maintenance and repair costs that are often overlooked in budgeting. From regular upkeep tasks like cleaning and landscaping to unexpected repairs such as plumbing issues or roof leaks, these expenses can add up over time. Allocate a portion of your budget to a home maintenance fund to cover these unforeseen costs.

2. Subscriptions And Memberships:

While many people remember to include major monthly subscriptions like streaming services, gym memberships, or cable bills in their budget, smaller subscriptions and memberships are often overlooked. These can include magazine subscriptions, software subscriptions, online courses, or even subscription boxes. Review your bank statements to identify any recurring expenses that you may have forgotten.

3. Medical Expenses:

Medical expenses, including copayments, deductibles, and prescription costs, are often underestimated or forgotten when budgeting. Additionally, it's crucial to plan for unexpected medical emergencies or unplanned doctor visits. Consider setting aside a portion of your budget for medical expenses or exploring health insurance options that suit your needs.

4. Car Maintenance And Repairs:

Car owners sometimes overlook the ongoing costs associated with maintaining and repairing their vehicles. Budget for regular oil changes, tire rotations, and inspections, as well as unexpected repairs like engine issues or brake replacements. Setting aside funds for car-related expenses can help you avoid financial strain when these inevitable costs arise.

5. Pet Expenses:

If you have furry companions, don't forget to budget for their needs. This includes pet food, grooming, vaccinations, annual check-ups, and unexpected veterinary expenses. Owning a pet comes with financial responsibilities, so make sure to factor these costs into your budget.

6. Gifts And Celebrations:

Birthdays, holidays, weddings, and other special occasions can lead to unexpected expenses if not properly budgeted for. Account for gifts, party supplies, decorations, and travel expenses associated with attending events. Planning ahead and setting a separate budget category for gifts and celebrations can help you avoid last-minute financial strain.

7. Homeowners Or Renters Insurance:

Insurance coverage for your home is often a requirement, but its cost can be forgotten in budgeting. Include your monthly insurance premiums in your budget to ensure you have adequate coverage and protection for your property and belongings.

8. Personal Care And Beauty:

Personal care expenses, such as haircuts, salon visits, skincare products, and grooming supplies, are often overlooked in budgeting. These costs can vary depending on your preferences and lifestyle. By including them in your budget, you can maintain your personal care routines without straining your finances.

9. Seasonal Expenses:

Seasonal expenses, like holiday decorations, winter clothing, summer activities, or back-to-school supplies, are often forgotten until they become immediate needs. Anticipate these expenses by allocating a portion of your budget each month to a seasonal fund. This way, you'll be financially prepared when the time comes.

In conclusion, overlooking certain expenses in your household budget can have significant consequences for your financial well-being. By addressing and including these commonly forgotten expenses in your budgeting process, you can achieve better financial stability, avoid unnecessary stress, and make informed decisions about your finances.

Throughout this article, we have explored nine commonly overlooked expenses that can have a substantial impact on your budget. These expenses include home maintenance and repairs, subscriptions and memberships, medical expenses, car maintenance and repairs, pet expenses, gifts and celebrations, homeowners' or renters' insurance, personal care and beauty, and seasonal expenses.

By being aware of these expenses and proactively allocating funds for them, you can ensure that your budget accurately reflects your financial reality. This will help you avoid unexpected financial strains, maintain control over your finances, and work towards achieving your financial goals.

Remember, budgeting is an ongoing process that requires regular review and adjustment. As your financial circumstances change and new expenses arise, it's important to revisit your budget and make necessary revisions to accommodate these changes. By staying proactive and adaptable, you can stay on top of your financial obligations and make informed decisions about your money.

Incorporating these commonly forgotten expenses into your budgeting process is a proactive step towards financial empowerment. By taking control of your finances and being mindful of all the costs involved, you can achieve greater financial resilience, reduce financial stress, and work towards a more secure future.

So, take the time to review your current budget, identify any overlooked expenses, and make the necessary adjustments. With a comprehensive understanding of your financial obligations, you can confidently navigate through life's financial challenges and pave the way for long-term financial success.

Start today by implementing these budgeting strategies, and watch as you gain more control over your finances, reduce financial surprises, and achieve greater peace of mind on your financial journey.

CHAPTER 11.

SMART MONEY MANAGEMENT: 7 EASY TIPS TO AVOID CREDIT CARD DEBT AND STAY FINANCIALLY SECURE

In today's fast-paced and consumer-driven world, credit cards have become an integral part of our financial landscape. They offer convenience, flexibility, and the ability to make purchases even when funds are tight. However, if not managed properly, credit cards can quickly become a double-edged sword, leading to overwhelming debt and financial stress.

The allure of instant gratification and the ease of swiping a card can make it tempting to overspend beyond our means. Credit card debt can pile up, and before we know it, we find ourselves trapped in a cycle of high-interest payments and struggling to make ends meet. But fear not, because, with a little smart money management and discipline, you can avoid falling into this debt trap and stay financially secure.

In this comprehensive guide, we will share seven easy-to-implement tips that can help you avoid credit card debt and establish healthy financial habits. By following these practical strategies, you will gain the confidence and knowledge to make informed decisions about your credit card usage while staying in control of your finances.

Whether you're just starting to use credit cards or have had some past struggles, this guide is designed to empower you with the tools and knowledge to stay ahead of credit card debt. From creating a realistic budget and paying off balances in full to monitoring statements and seeking professional advice when needed, each tip is designed to provide actionable steps towards financial security.

So, if you're ready to take charge of your financial well-being, let's dive in and discover how you can navigate the world of credit cards while maintaining your financial stability and peace of mind.

1. Create A Realistic Budget:

A crucial step towards avoiding credit card debt is establishing a realistic budget. Start by evaluating your income, expenses, and financial goals. Allocate a specific portion of your income for necessities such as rent/mortgage, utilities, and groceries. Set aside another portion for savings and emergency funds. Finally, allocate a reasonable amount for discretionary spending. By having a clear budget, you'll have a better understanding of your financial limitations and be less likely to overspend on credit.

2. Pay Off Balances In Full:

One of the most effective ways to avoid credit card debt is to pay off your balances in full each month. Carrying balances forward accrues interest charges, which can quickly add up. Make it a habit to pay your credit card bill in its entirety before the due date. This way, you'll avoid interest charges and develop responsible payment habits.

3. Limit The Number Of Credit Cards:

Having multiple credit cards can tempt you to overspend and accumulate debt. It's wise to limit the number of credit cards you own to avoid spreading your finances too thin. Evaluate your needs and select cards that align with your spending habits and offer favorable terms, such as low-interest rates or rewards programs.

4. Use Credit Cards For Planned Purchases:

Credit cards can provide convenience and security, especially for online transactions and travel. However, it's essential to use credit cards for planned purchases that you have budgeted for. Avoid using credit cards for impulsive or unnecessary expenses, as this can quickly lead to debt. Stick to your budget and consider alternative payment methods for unplanned purchases.

5. Monitor Your Credit Card Statements Regularly:

Staying vigilant about monitoring your credit card statements is crucial to identify any unauthorized transactions or errors promptly. Regularly review your statements for accuracy and report any discrepancies to your credit card issuer immediately. By being proactive, you can prevent fraudulent charges and address billing issues promptly.

6. Resist Minimum Payments:

Paying only the minimum amount due on your credit card may seem convenient, but it can trap you in a cycle of debt. Minimum payments mainly cover interest charges, prolonging the time it takes to pay off the principal balance. Instead, strive to pay more than the minimum payment each month, focusing on reducing the outstanding balance and minimizing interest charges.

7. Seek Professional Advice:

If you find yourself struggling with credit card debt or facing financial challenges, seeking professional advice can be invaluable. Consider consulting with a certified credit counsellor or financial advisor who specializes in debt management. They can provide guidance on creating a customized debt repayment plan, negotiating with creditors, and improving your overall financial situation.

By implementing these seven easy tips for smart money management, you can steer clear of credit card debt and maintain financial stability. Remember, establishing a realistic budget, paying off balances in full, and being mindful of your credit card usage are key habits to develop. Monitor your statements regularly, resist making only minimum payments, and seek professional advice when needed. By practicing responsible financial habits, you can achieve financial security and build a strong foundation for a bright financial future. Avoiding credit card debt and maintaining financial security requires commitment, discipline, and smart money management. By implementing the seven easy tips outlined in this guide, you have the power to take control of your finances and build a strong foundation for a secure future.

Remember, creating a realistic budget and sticking to it is the cornerstone of responsible financial management. Paying off your credit card balances in full each month helps you avoid interest charges and develop good payment habits. Limiting the number of credit cards and using them only for planned purchases keeps your spending in check.

Regularly monitoring your credit card statements and promptly addressing any discrepancies or errors ensures that you're in control of your financial transactions. Resisting the allure of minimum payments and striving to pay more than the minimum amount due accelerates your debt repayment and minimizes interest charges.

And finally, don't hesitate to seek professional advice if you find yourself overwhelmed by credit card debt or facing financial challenges. Certified credit counsellors and financial advisors can provide personalized guidance and support to help you regain control of your finances.

By applying these tips consistently and making responsible financial decisions, you can avoid credit card debt, enjoy peace of mind, and pave the way towards a financially secure future. Remember, you hold the key to your financial success, and with these strategies, you can confidently navigate the credit card landscape and achieve your financial goals.

CHAPTER 12.

TRAVELING THE WORLD
ON A LIMITED BUDGET

In a world that often seems to prioritize opulence in travel, the idea of embarking on a global adventure with limited financial resources might feel like an audacious pursuit. However, contrary to popular belief, the allure of wanderlust doesn't have to be synonymous with exorbitant costs. It's time to debunk the myth that globe-trotting requires a bottomless bank account and embrace the notion that with strategic planning, resourcefulness, and a genuine passion for exploration, you can traverse the world on a shoestring budget.

As we delve into the intricacies of budget travel in this comprehensive guide, imagine a journey where the emphasis is not on the price tag but on the richness of experiences, the authenticity of interactions, and the depth of cultural immersion. Beyond the glossy brochures and luxury resorts lies a world waiting to be discovered by those who are willing to approach travel as an art, blending financial acumen with an insatiable curiosity for the unknown.

So, if the thought of exploring distant lands, engaging with diverse cultures, and creating lasting memories appeals to you, fear not the limitations of your budget. This guide is your compass, leading you through the avenues of economical travel, offering insights into the art of budgeting, the wonders of the sharing economy, the allure of off-the-beaten-path destinations, the rewards of volunteering, the wisdom of efficient packing, the benefits of public transportation, and the delights of local cuisine and markets.

As we unravel the secrets of thrifty globetrotting, prepare to redefine the way you perceive travel. It's not merely about reaching a destination; it's about the journey itself—the people you meet, the stories you collect, and the transformation that occurs within. Buckle up for a travel revolution, where the limitations of your budget become the catalyst for a more profound, authentic, and fulfilling adventure. Welcome to the world of budget travel—where the pursuit of dreams and the quest for discovery know no financial boundaries.

1. The Art Of Traval Budgeting:

Embarking on a journey around the world with a limited budget requires a solid foundation, and that foundation is built upon the art of budgeting. Before setting foot on foreign soil, take the time to meticulously plan and allocate your finances. Start by creating a comprehensive travel budget that encompasses all potential expenses, including accommodation, transportation, meals, activities, and unforeseen costs.

Utilize budgeting tools and apps that are designed for travelers, such as Trail Wallet or Mint. These apps help you track your spending in real-time, enabling you to stay within your budgetary limits. Regularly updating your budget as you travel ensures that you are aware of your financial standing and can make informed decisions on where to allocate your funds.

Consider breaking down your budget on a daily or weekly basis, allowing for flexibility in spending across different phases of your journey. This granular approach helps you maintain financial discipline while adapting to the dynamic nature of travel.

It's also essential to research and plan for destination-specific costs. Recognize that the cost of living varies from place to place, and by understanding the local economy, you can make informed choices that align with your budget. Prioritize experiences that resonate with you, and allocate resources accordingly.

Mastering the art of budgeting isn't just about restriction; it's about empowerment. It gives you control over your finances, allowing you to make the most of your resources and ensuring that you can sustain your travels for an extended period. With a well-crafted budget as your guide, you can navigate the world with confidence, knowing that every dollar spent contributes to the enrichment of your global adventure.

2. Embracing The Sharing Economy:

In the realm of budget travel, one of the most impactful shifts in recent years has been the rise of the sharing economy. This innovative concept involves sharing resources, services, and accommodations with others, creating a more collaborative and cost-effective approach to travel. Platforms like Airbnb and Couchsurfing have become game-changers for budget-conscious adventurers.

Rather than opting for traditional hotels, which can be expensive, many travelers now explore the sharing economy for unique and affordable accommodation options. Airbnb allows individuals to rent out their homes or spare rooms, providing travelers with a local experience at a fraction of the cost. This not only saves money but also fosters a more personalized and authentic connection with the destination.

Couchsurfing takes the concept even further by connecting travelers with locals who are willing to offer free accommodations. This not only drastically reduces lodging expenses but also opens the door to cultural exchange, as hosts often share insights and recommendations, turning your stay into a richer, more immersive experience.

Beyond accommodations, the sharing economy extends to transportation. Ride-sharing services like Uber and Lyft offer cost-effective alternatives to traditional taxis. Additionally, car-sharing platforms like Turo allow travelers to rent vehicles directly from locals, often at lower rates than traditional rental agencies.

Embracing the sharing economy in travel is not just about saving money; it's about fostering connections, breaking down barriers, and immersing oneself in the genuine fabric of a destination. It's a paradigm shift that empowers both hosts and travelers, turning the journey into a shared experience that goes beyond the transactional nature of traditional travel services. As budget-conscious adventurers increasingly embrace this collaborative approach, the sharing economy continues to redefine the way we explore the world.

3. Exploring Off-The-Beaten-Path Destinations:

Popular tourist destinations often come with a hefty price tag. Instead of following the well-trodden path, explore off-the-beaten-track destinations that are not only more affordable but also provide a more authentic cultural experience. Venture into small towns and villages where you can engage with locals and savor the true essence of a region.

4. Volunteering And Skill Trading:

Traveling with a purpose not only enriches your experience but also can significantly reduce your expenses. Explore volunteer opportunities through platforms like Workaway or WWOOF, where you can exchange your skills for accommodation and meals. Whether teaching a language, assisting with community projects, or working on sustainable farms, these experiences not only contribute positively to the places you visit but also create lasting memories.

5. Packing Efficiently And Thoughtfully:

Packing efficiently is an art that budget travelers swear by. Opt for versatile clothing that can be mixed and matched, reducing the need to pack an outfit for every occasion. Embrace the philosophy of "less is more," packing only the essentials and leaving room for souvenirs or items collected along the way. Invest in lightweight, durable luggage and consider the practicality of each item before it earns a spot in your backpack.

6. Utilizing Public Transportation:

Public transportation is the unsung hero of budget travel. Opt for buses, trains, and local transport instead of expensive taxis or rental cars. Many cities offer discount cards or passes for public transportation, providing a cost-effective way to explore your surroundings. Engaging with locals on public transit also offers an authentic glimpse into everyday life, fostering a deeper connection with the destination.

7. Navigating Local Cuisine And Markets:

Indulging in local cuisine is a vital aspect of travel, and it can be budget-friendly if approached wisely. Dine at local markets and street stalls, where you can savor authentic flavors at a fraction of the cost of fancy restaurants. Experiment with regional specialties and engage with vendors to gain insights into the local food culture. Additionally, carry a reusable water bottle to save on the expense of buying bottled water throughout your journey.

Embarking on a global adventure with a limited budget requires a blend of financial acumen, open-mindedness, and a willingness to step off the beaten path. By mastering the art of budgeting, embracing the sharing economy, exploring off-the-beaten-path destinations, volunteering or trading skills, packing efficiently, utilizing public transportation, and navigating local cuisine and markets, you can unlock the door to a world of affordable and enriching travel experiences. So, lace up your travel shoes, adjust your backpack, and get ready to explore the world in a way that leaves both your heart and wallet full.

CHAPTER 13.

ACCELERATE DEBT REPAYMENT: UNVEILING EFFECTIVE 03 TRICKS TO PAY OFF YOUR DEBT FASTER

Debt can be a heavy burden that affects your financial well-being and limits your freedom. Whether it's credit card debt, student loans, or other forms of borrowing, finding ways to pay off your debt faster can provide immense relief and set you on the path to financial freedom. In this article, we will reveal three effective tricks to help you accelerate your debt repayment journey. By implementing these strategies, you can regain control of your finances and achieve debt-free living sooner than you thought possible.

Living with debt can be overwhelming, causing stress and anxiety. It may feel like a never-ending cycle, with interest piling up and minimum payments barely making a dent in the principal balance. However, it's important to remember that you have the power to take charge of your financial situation and work towards a debt-free future.

The key to paying off your debt faster lies in implementing proven strategies and making conscious financial decisions. By employing the right techniques, you can not only expedite your debt repayment but also save money on interest payments and improve your overall financial health.

In this article, we will explore three powerful tricks that can help you accelerate your debt repayment journey. These strategies involve creating a comprehensive debt repayment plan, trimming expenses and increasing income, and negotiating with creditors. By following these tactics, you can make significant progress towards becoming debt-free and achieving financial peace of mind.

Remember, paying off debt requires commitment and persistence. It may not always be an easy journey, but every step you take towards debt freedom brings you closer to financial independence. Let's dive into the three effective tricks that will empower you to pay off your debt faster and build a solid foundation for a brighter financial future.

1. Create A Comprehensive Debt Repayment Plan:

The first step towards paying off your debt faster is to create a well-structured and comprehensive debt repayment plan. Start by listing all your debts, including outstanding balances, interest rates, and minimum monthly payments. This gives you a clear overview of your financial obligations. Next, identify the most suitable debt repayment strategy for your situation.

A) Debt Snowball Method:

This approach involves paying off your debts in order from the smallest to the largest balance. By focusing on the smallest debt first, you gain momentum and motivation as you eliminate individual debts one by one. As each debt is paid off, roll the amount you were paying towards that debt into the next one on your list.

B) Debt Avalanche Method:

With this strategy, you prioritize paying off debts with the highest interest rates first. By tackling high-interest debts aggressively, you minimize the amount of interest accruing over time. Once the debt with the highest interest rate is paid off, shift your focus to the next highest interest rate debt.

C) Debt Consolidation:

If you have multiple high-interest debts, consider consolidating them into a single loan with a lower interest rate. This simplifies your repayment process and can potentially save you money on interest payments. However, be cautious and evaluate the terms and fees associated with the consolidation option to ensure it truly benefits your situation.

2. Create A Comprehensive Debt Repayment Plan:

The first step towards paying off your debt faster is to create a well-structured and comprehensive debt repayment plan. Start by listing all your debts, including outstanding balances, interest rates, and minimum monthly payments. This gives you a clear overview of your financial obligations. Next, identify the most suitable debt repayment strategy for your situation.

Simultaneously, explore ways to increase your income. Consider taking up a part-time job, freelancing, or pursuing a side hustle to generate extra cash. Channel these additional earnings towards your debt repayment plan, helping you make larger payments and shorten the repayment timeline.

3. Negotiate With Creditors:

Don't underestimate the power of negotiation when it comes to debt repayment. Contact your creditors and explore the possibility of negotiating better terms. This could involve requesting lower interest rates, waiving certain fees, or establishing a more manageable repayment plan. Creditors may be willing to work with you if they see your commitment to repaying the debt.

Additionally, if you're struggling to meet your minimum payments, seek professional assistance from credit counselling agencies. They can help negotiate with creditors on your behalf and provide guidance on managing your debt effectively.

Paying off your debt faster requires determination, discipline, and a well-executed plan. By implementing the tricks outlined in this article, you can accelerate your debt repayment journey and reclaim your financial freedom. Create a comprehensive debt repayment plan tailored to your situation, trim expenses, increase your income, and negotiate with creditors when necessary. Remember, every small step towards debt freedom counts, and with persistence, you can achieve your goal of living a debt-free life. Take control of your finances today and embark on the path to a brighter financial future.

Creating a comprehensive debt repayment plan tailored to your situation is the first step towards accelerated debt repayment. Whether you choose the debt snowball method, debt avalanche method, or debt consolidation, having a clear strategy in place helps you stay focused and motivated throughout the journey.

Trimming expenses and increasing your income are crucial elements in expediting your debt repayment. By evaluating your spending habits, identifying areas where you can cut back, and exploring opportunities for additional income, you can free up more funds to put towards your debt. Every dollar saved and earned brings you closer to financial freedom.

Don't underestimate the power of negotiation when it comes to paying off your debt faster. Contact your creditors and explore the possibility of negotiating better terms. By demonstrating your commitment to repaying the debt and seeking assistance from credit counselling agencies if needed, you can potentially secure lower interest rates or more manageable repayment plans.

Remember, the road to debt freedom may not always be easy, and setbacks may occur along the way. However, with determination, discipline, and the tricks outlined in this article, you have the tools to overcome challenges and achieve your goal of living a debt-free life.

Celebrate every milestone and progress you make along your debt repayment journey. Each payment made brings you closer to financial independence and a future free from the constraints of debt. Stay focused, stay motivated, and embrace the financial freedom that awaits you.

Take charge of your financial situation today and embark on the path to a brighter future. Accelerate your debt repayment, regain control of your finances, and set yourself up for long-term financial success. You have the power to shape your financial destiny. Start today and enjoy the journey to a debt-free life.

CHAPTER 14.

UNDERSTANDING THE DISTINCTION: BAD DEBT VS. GOOD DEBT EXPLAINED

D ebt is a concept that is often associated with negative connotations. The thought of owing money can evoke feelings of stress and anxiety. However, it's important to realize that not all debt is created equal. Understanding the difference between bad debt and good debt is essential for making informed financial decisions that can shape your long-term financial well-being.

Bad debt refers to borrowing that does not contribute to your financial growth or generate potential returns. It typically involves purchases that quickly lose value or do not appreciate over time. Examples of bad debt include high-interest credit card debt incurred from impulse purchases, personal loans for non-essential items, or payday loans that carry exorbitant interest rates. Bad debt can become a burden, making it difficult to achieve your financial goals and build wealth.

On the other hand, good debt is an investment in your future or an asset that has the potential to appreciate over time. This type of debt can contribute to your long-term financial success. Examples of good debt include student loans used to obtain a valuable degree, a mortgage for purchasing a home, or a business loan to start or expand a profitable venture. Good debt can provide opportunities for growth, enhance your earning potential, and contribute to wealth accumulation.

By gaining a deeper understanding of bad debt and good debt, you can make informed decisions about borrowing and prioritize your financial well-being. In this blog post, we will explore the characteristics and implications of each type of debt, discuss strategies for managing debt effectively, and provide tips for leveraging good debt to build a solid financial foundation. Let's dive into the distinctions between bad debt and good debt, empowering you to make wise financial choices and achieve long-term financial success.

1. Defining Bad Debt:

Bad debt refers to borrowing that does not contribute to your long-term financial well-being or generate potential returns. It is often associated with purchases that quickly depreciate in value or do not appreciate over time. Examples of bad debt include high-interest credit card debt, personal loans for discretionary spending, or impulse purchases financed through loans. Bad debt can lead to a cycle of minimum payments that barely cover the interest, making it difficult to make significant progress in paying down the principal balance.

2. The Impact Of Bad Debt:

Carrying excessive bad debt can have significant negative consequences on your financial health. High-interest rates associated with bad debt can result in substantial interest payments, prolonging the time it takes to pay off the debt and increasing the overall cost. Bad debt can also negatively affect your credit score, making it harder to obtain favorable interest rates for future borrowing. The stress of dealing with bad debt can impact your overall well-being, causing anxiety and limiting your ability to save and invest for the future.

3. Understanding Good Debt:

Good debt, on the other hand, represents borrowing that can contribute to your long-term financial success or appreciates in value over time. It is often associated with investments in education, homeownership, or business ventures. Student loans used to obtain a valuable degree or professional certification can be considered good debt since they enhance your earning potential and future career opportunities. Mortgages for purchasing a home are also considered good debt because they allow you to build equity and potentially benefit from property appreciation. Business loans used to start or expand a profitable venture can be classified as good debt if they generate income and contribute to long-term financial growth.

4. The Benefits Of Good Debt:

Good debt offers several benefits that can contribute to your financial well-being. Education, for example, can lead to higher-paying job opportunities and increased earning potential. Homeownership provides stability, the potential for equity accumulation, and certain tax benefits. Business loans can fuel entrepreneurial ventures and create opportunities for growth and wealth creation. Responsible management of good debt, including making timely payments, can also positively impact your credit score, making it easier to secure future loans at favorable terms.

5. Assessing Risk And Managing Debt:

While good debt can be beneficial, it is important to assess risk and ensure that your borrowing aligns with your financial capabilities and goals. Careful consideration of interest rates, repayment terms, and the potential return on investment is essential when taking on any debt. Proper budgeting, monitoring spending habits, and creating a repayment plan is crucial for managing both bad debt and good debt effectively.

6. Striking A Balance:

Striking a balance between managing bad debt and leveraging good debt is key to maintaining a healthy financial life. Minimizing bad debt by prioritizing debt repayment, reducing unnecessary expenses, and avoiding unnecessary borrowing is essential. At the same time, strategic use of good debt can create opportunities for growth and financial advancement. It is important to find the right balance that aligns with your financial goals, risk tolerance, and overall financial well-being.

When it comes to distinguishing between bad debt and good debt, there are important factors to consider and precautions to take. Here are key aspects to be careful about when it comes to bad debt and good debt:

A. Interest Rates:

Pay close attention to the interest rates associated with any debt you take on. Bad debt often carries high-interest rates, making it more expensive to borrow and harder to pay off. Good debt, on the other hand, may have lower interest rates, but it's still important to compare rates and choose the most favorable options.

B. Repayment Terms:

Understand the repayment terms for any debt you incur. Bad debt may come with shorter repayment periods and higher monthly payments, which can put a strain on your budget. Good debt may offer more flexible repayment terms, allowing you to manage your payments more effectively. However, always ensure that you can comfortably meet the repayment obligations for any debt you take on.

C. Risk Assessment:

Assess the risk involved in taking on any debt. Bad debt often carries higher risk, as it is associated with purchases that depreciate or lack potential returns. Good debt carries its own risks, such as the potential for housing market fluctuations or business ventures that may not succeed. Evaluate the potential risks and weigh them against the potential benefits before taking on any debt.

D. Financial Goals:

Consider how the debt aligns with your financial goals. Bad debt rarely contributes to long-term financial success, while good debt can be an investment in your future. Prioritize debt that helps you achieve your financial goals, such as education that enhances your earning potential or a mortgage that builds equity.

E. Debt Management:

Be cautious about managing your debt load. Too much bad

debt can quickly become overwhelming, making it harder to pay off and affecting your financial well-being. Strive to minimize bad debt and manage good debt responsibly by making regular payments and avoiding excessive borrowing.

F. Individual Circumstances:

Remember that everyone's financial situation is unique. What may be considered a good debt for one person may not be suitable for another. Take into account your income, expenses, risk tolerance, and overall financial health when deciding whether to take on any type of debt.

By being careful and thoughtful about these factors, you can navigate the distinction between bad debt and good debt more effectively. Prioritize debt that aligns with your financial goals, assess risks, and manage your debt responsibly to build a solid financial foundation.

Understanding the distinction between bad debt and good debt is crucial for taking control of your financial future. While bad debt can be burdensome and hinder your progress, good debt can be a strategic tool for achieving your financial goals and building wealth. By recognizing the characteristics and implications of each type of debt, you can make informed borrowing decisions and take steps towards financial freedom.

Managing bad debt is essential for regaining financial stability. By prioritizing debt repayment, implementing strategies to reduce interest payments, and avoiding unnecessary borrowing, you can alleviate the negative impact of bad debt on your finances. This may involve creating a budget, negotiating with creditors, or seeking professional assistance to develop a debt repayment plan.

At the same time, leveraging good debt strategically can open doors to opportunities and accelerate your financial growth. By investing in education, homeownership, or business ventures, you can enhance your earning potential and create long-term wealth. It's important, however, to approach good debt with caution and ensure that it aligns with your financial goals and ability to repay.

Ultimately, achieving financial well-being requires a balanced approach to debt management. Minimizing bad debt, harnessing the power of good debt, and practicing responsible borrowing habits are essential components of a sound financial strategy. By incorporating these principles into your financial decisions, you can build a solid foundation for a secure and prosperous future.

CHAPTER 15.

DEBT MANAGEMENT: 7 POWERFUL SECRETS FOR TAKING CONTROL OF YOUR FINANCES

In today's fast-paced world, managing debt has become a crucial skill for achieving financial stability and peace of mind. With various financial commitments like student loans, credit card debt, and mortgages, it's easy to feel overwhelmed and buried under a mountain of financial obligations. However, the good news is that mastering the art of debt management is not an insurmountable task. By employing effective strategies and adopting a proactive approach, you can take control of your finances and pave the way towards a debt-free future.

In this comprehensive blog post, we will delve into seven powerful debt management strategies that will equip you with the tools and knowledge to regain control of your financial situation. Whether you're struggling with mounting credit card bills or feeling the weight of student loans, these proven strategies will guide you towards better financial health.

The journey to debt freedom begins with understanding the nature of your debts. By creating a detailed list of all your financial obligations, including balances, interest rates, and minimum monthly payments, you will gain a clear and realistic picture of where you stand. Armed with this knowledge, you can develop a strategic plan tailored to your financial circumstances.

A critical aspect of effective debt management is the creation of a realistic budget. Your budget will act as a roadmap, allowing you to allocate your income wisely and prioritize debt repayment. Through careful analysis of your income and expenses, you'll identify areas where you can cut back and allocate more funds towards paying off debts.

Prioritizing debts can make a significant impact on your financial journey. By focusing on high-interest debts first, you'll save money on interest charges and accelerate your path to debt freedom. We'll explore how to structure your repayment plan to maximize its impact, helping you gain momentum in your journey towards a debt-free life.

Debt consolidation is another powerful tool in your debt management arsenal. By consolidating multiple debts into a single, lower-interest loan, you can simplify your repayment process and potentially reduce your overall interest burden. We'll walk you through the benefits and considerations of debt consolidation, so you can make an informed decision.

While navigating the world of debt, it's crucial to maintain open lines of communication with your creditors. Negotiating with them can yield favorable outcomes, such as modified payment plans or settlements. Our guide will provide you with tips and strategies for effective communication, empowering you to find viable solutions in challenging situations.

In addition to focusing on debt repayment, we'll emphasize the importance of building an emergency fund. This financial safety net will shield you from falling back into debt when unexpected expenses arise. We'll discuss how to establish and grow your emergency fund to provide stability during uncertain times.

For those feeling overwhelmed or unsure of their next steps, seeking professional help can be a game-changer. Financial advisors and debt counsellors can offer personalized advice and tailored strategies to address your unique financial challenges. We'll explore when and how to seek professional assistance to ensure your debt management journey stays on track.

Remember, mastering the art of debt management is a journey that requires dedication and discipline. By following these seven powerful strategies and committing to proactive financial practices, you'll be well on your way to taking control of your finances and securing a brighter, debt-free future. Let's embark on this transformative journey together!

1. Understand Your Debt:

The first step in effective debt management is gaining a complete understanding of your debt. Create a list of all your debts, including balances, interest rates, and minimum monthly payments. This will give you a clear picture of where you stand and help you prioritize your repayment strategy.

2. Create A Realistic Budget:

A well-thought-out budget is the backbone of successful debt management. Analyze your income and expenses to identify areas where you can cut back and allocate more funds towards debt repayment. Having a budget will also prevent overspending and ensure you stay on track with your financial goals.

3. Prioritize High-Interest Debts:

Tackling high-interest debts first can save you a significant amount of money in the long run. Make a plan to pay off debts with higher interest rates while making minimum payments on others. As you eliminate each debt, redirect the funds towards the next one on your list.

4. Consider Debt Consolidation:

Dealing with multiple debts and interest rates can be overwhelming. Debt consolidation can simplify the process by combining all your debts into a single loan with a lower interest rate. This will not only reduce your monthly payments but also help you save on interest charges.

5. Negotiate With Creditors:

If you're struggling to make payments, don't hesitate to reach out to your creditors. Many creditors are willing to work with you to create a more manageable payment plan or negotiate a settlement. Being proactive and communicating your situation can help you avoid defaulting on your debts.

6. Build An Emergency Fund:

Creating an emergency fund is essential to avoid falling back into debt in case of unexpected expenses. Aim to save at least three to six months' worth of living expenses in a separate account, which will act as a safety net during tough times.

7. Seek Professional Help:

If you find yourself overwhelmed with debt and unsure of how to proceed, consider seeking professional help. Financial advisors and debt counsellors can provide personalized advice and guidance tailored to your specific situation, helping you make informed decisions on your journey to debt freedom.

You've reached the end of this empowering journey towards mastering the art of debt management. By now, you've learned seven powerful strategies that can help you take control of your finances and lead you to a debt-free future. As you reflect on the insights shared in this blog post, remember that the road to financial freedom is within your grasp, and with dedication and perseverance, you can achieve your goals.

Understanding your debts and creating a realistic budget have laid the foundation for your debt management plan. By taking a comprehensive look at your financial situation, you've gained valuable insights into your debts, allowing you to prioritize them strategically. Armed with a well-structured budget, you've taken the first step towards allocating your resources effectively and optimizing your financial progress.

The journey to debt freedom requires focus and determination, especially when dealing with high-interest debts. Through disciplined efforts and commitment to repayment, you can make steady progress towards reducing your debt burden. Celebrate each milestone, no matter how small, as they signify significant steps towards financial independence.

Debt consolidation has emerged as a powerful tool to streamline your debt management process. By combining multiple debts into a single, manageable loan, you've simplified your financial landscape and taken control of your debt repayment journey. With this newfound structure, you can stay focused on your goal with reduced complexity and potentially lower interest rates.

Negotiating with creditors has empowered you to take charge of your financial destiny. Effective communication and proactive engagement can lead to mutually beneficial solutions, including modified payment plans or settlements. As you build and nurture these relationships, you'll find that creditors are more willing to work with you during challenging times.

Building an emergency fund has provided you with a safety net during unexpected events. With financial stability, you can avoid sliding back into debt when faced with unforeseen expenses or emergencies. Your emergency fund is a testament to your financial prudence and readiness to tackle life's uncertainties.

Lastly, seeking professional help is a sign of strength and resourcefulness. Financial advisors and debt counsellors are valuable allies on your journey to debt freedom. Their expertise and personalized guidance can help you navigate complex financial situations and maintain the right course towards financial success.

As you continue on your debt management journey, remember that progress may not always be linear. There might be setbacks and challenges along the way, but do not be discouraged. Persevere, stay focused on your goals, and remember the lessons learned in this blog post.

Your commitment to mastering the art of debt management will not only improve your financial situation but also foster a greater sense of empowerment and control over your life. As you apply these strategies and develop healthy financial habits, you'll witness the transformation of your financial landscape, opening doors to new opportunities and possibilities.

With these powerful tools in your arsenal, you can reshape your financial future. Take each step with confidence and belief in your ability to overcome any obstacle. Embrace the journey, celebrate your successes, and keep your sights firmly set on the ultimate prize: a debt-free life and a brighter financial future.

Remember, you are in charge of your financial destiny, and you have the power to achieve financial freedom. So go forth, armed with knowledge and determination, and make your dreams of a debt-free and financially secure life a reality. The path to success is before you – seize it with unwavering resolve and ambition. Happy debt management!

CHAPTER 16.

SMART HOME BUYING UNVEILED: AVOID THESE 4 COSTLY MISTAKES FOR A SMOOTH PURCHASE PROCESS

The journey towards homeownership is a monumental chapter in the book of life, where aspirations meet reality, and dreams find a place to call home. The prospect of owning a piece of real estate is exhilarating, yet beneath the excitement lies a complex landscape laden with potential pitfalls. In the realm of home buying, knowledge is power, and avoiding common mistakes can be the key to a seamless and gratifying experience.

Welcome to a comprehensive guide that sheds light on the art of intelligent home buying—an exploration that unveils four critical mistakes you must steer clear of for a purchase process that glides effortlessly towards success. From understanding the significance of pre-approval to unravelling the imperative of a thorough home inspection, from navigating beyond the purchase price to embracing a strategic perspective on future resale value, this guide serves as your compass in the often-intricate world of real estate.

Embark with us on a journey of discovery, where we equip you with insights and strategies to navigate the home buying landscape with confidence. Unveil the secrets of making informed decisions, and empower yourself to sidestep pitfalls that can transform your dream home into an unexpected challenge. As we unravel the intricacies of these four costly mistakes, you'll gain a deeper understanding of how to approach the home buying process intelligently and set the stage for a future of comfort, joy, and financial security.

1. Skipping Pre-Approval: A Foundation For Informed Decisions

One of the gravest mistakes you can make as a homebuyer is to skip the pre-approval stage. It's like embarking on a journey without a map. Pre-approval is a process where you consult a mortgage lender who reviews your financial history, credit score, and income to determine how much you can borrow. Armed with a pre-approval letter, you gain a clear understanding of your budget and present yourself as a serious and qualified buyer to sellers.

Without pre-approval, you might fall in love with a property that's beyond your financial reach, leading to disappointment and wasted time. Pre-approval sets the foundation for an informed home search, allowing you to focus on properties that align with your budget and avoid the heartbreak of falling for a home you can't afford.

2. Neglecting A Thorough Home Inspection: Unveiling Hidden Issues

Buying a home is an investment, and like any investment, due diligence is essential. Neglecting a comprehensive home inspection can be a costly mistake that haunts you long after the purchase. A home inspection involves a professional evaluating the property's structural elements, systems, and components, unveiling any potential issues that might not be immediately apparent.

An inspector's trained eye can identify problems such as plumbing leaks, electrical issues, mould, and even structural concerns. Their detailed report provides you with valuable insights, enabling you to negotiate with the seller for repairs or a price reduction. Skipping or rushing through this step can lead to unexpected expenses and regrets. Investing in a thorough inspection is an investment in your peace of mind and financial well-being.

3. Underestimating Total Costs: Beyond The Purchase Price

Homebuyers often focus on the purchase price as the primary expense, but this is just the tip of the iceberg. Numerous other costs are associated with buying a home that can catch you off guard if not appropriately considered.

Closing costs, for instance, encompass a range of fees, including appraisal fees, title insurance, attorney fees, and more. These costs can add up to a significant amount, so it's crucial to factor them into your budget. Additionally, ongoing expenses such as property taxes, homeowner's insurance, and potential homeowner association (HOA) fees should not be overlooked.

Furthermore, allocate funds for potential home improvements or renovations you might want to undertake after moving in. Underestimating these costs can strain your finances and lead to post-purchase stress.

4. Ignoring Future Resale Value: Planning For The Long-Term

While the home you're considering might meet your current needs and desires, it's essential to consider its future resale value. Life is dynamic, and circumstances can change, prompting you to sell the property. Ignoring this aspect can result in difficulties when you're ready to move on.

To ensure a solid investment, research the neighborhood's growth potential, school quality, and overall real estate market trends. A property located in an area with solid appreciation rates ensures that you not only enjoy your living space but also have a valuable asset that can appreciate over time.

A Thoughtful And Informed Home Purchase

In the grand tapestry of life, the decision to buy a home is a defining thread—a testament to your dreams, ambitions, and the place you envision creating a lifetime of experiences. As we reach the conclusion of this guide, we emphasize the pivotal importance of making informed decisions during your journey to homeownership. By steering clear of the four common yet avoidable mistakes—skipping pre-approval, neglecting home inspection, underestimating total costs, and disregarding future resale value—you have a smoother path towards turning your aspirations into reality.

Homeownership is more than a mere transaction; it's an investment in your future, both financially and emotionally. It's about finding that perfect enclave where you can craft stories, celebrate milestones, and find solace after a long day. Armed with the insights gained from this guide, you are better equipped to embark on this journey with confidence, awareness, and the ability to sidestep potential obstacles.

Remember that wisdom lies not only in knowing what to do but also in understanding what to avoid. While each step of the home-buying process is important, your ability to avoid pitfalls is equally crucial. Pre-approval lays the groundwork, home inspection offers clarity, considering total costs ensures financial stability, and thinking about future resale value safeguards your investment.

Consult experts, engage with professionals, and seek advice from those who have navigated this path before. The memories you create within the walls of your new home will be priceless, and your financial well-being is equally significant. Smart home buying requires a blend of intuition and prudence—an artful dance between emotions and logic.

As you embark on this odyssey, embrace the lessons shared here as your guiding stars. With each decision you make, you carve your path towards not just acquiring a property, but also creating a haven where your aspirations unfold. In homeownership, knowledge is your compass, and an informed journey promises a future defined by comfort, joy, and the fulfilment of your dreams. So go forth, armed with wisdom, and let your journey to homeownership be a true reflection of your hopes and aspirations.

CHAPTER 17.

POST-HOME PURCHASE UNVEILED: 7 THINGS TO EXPECT AFTER YOU BUY A HOME

The journey of purchasing a home is a remarkable endeavor that culminates in a moment of triumph—the moment when the keys to your new abode are finally in your hands. It's a culmination of dreams, aspirations, and hard work, marking the beginning of a new chapter in your life's story. Yet, as you step across the threshold of your newly acquired property, a new narrative unfolds—one that involves adjustment, exploration and the navigation of new experiences.

In this comprehensive guide, we delve into the often-unspoken aspects of post-home purchase life. Beyond the excitement of house hunting and negotiations lies a period of transition, where understanding what to expect is pivotal. Buying a home is not just about the transaction; it's about embracing a lifestyle, becoming a part of a community, and creating a haven that resonates with your identity.

In the following sections, we'll explore seven fundamental elements that you should be prepared for after purchasing a home. From the practicalities of budgeting and maintenance to the emotional aspects of settling in and personalizing your space, this guide will serve as your roadmap to navigating the post-purchase landscape with confidence and foresight.

As you embark on this new phase of your journey, remember that every aspect of homeownership is a part of your story. The adjustments you make, the memories you create, and the experiences you encounter are all threads woven into the tapestry of your life. So, let's dive into these seven key elements that await you after the exhilarating moment of acquiring your dream home. By understanding and embracing these factors, you'll be well-prepared for the adventure that lies ahead—a journey that transforms a house into a cherished home.

1. Settling In Takes Time

The thrill of moving into your dream home might make you eager to unpack, arrange furniture, and put down roots immediately. While enthusiasm is commendable, remember that settling in takes time. Adjusting to a new environment, mapping out the best arrangement for your space, and making your house truly feel like home will naturally unfold over days or even weeks. Give yourself the grace to adapt at your own pace.

2. Budgeting Beyond The Purchase

Owning a home comes with financial responsibilities beyond the initial purchase. In addition to mortgage payments, be prepared for ongoing expenses like property taxes, utility bills, homeowner association (HOA) fees (if applicable), and maintenance costs. Planning for these financial aspects ensures a seamless transition into the realm of homeownership.

3. Home Maintenance Is A Key

As the proud owner of a property, maintenance becomes a top priority. Regular upkeep, from changing air filters to tending to the garden, not only enhances your living experience but also preserves the value of your investment. Create a maintenance schedule and allocate resources to tackle tasks both big and small, ensuring your home remains a comfortable haven.

4. Navigating Neighborhood Dynamics

Your new neighborhood might have its own rhythm and dynamics that differ from your previous locale. Take time to explore, get to know your neighbors, and engage with local events. Being an active part of your community enhances your sense of belonging and contributes to a fulfilling homeownership experience.

5. Unexpected Surprises And Repairs

Even if you've had a thorough home inspection, surprises and repairs can still emerge. A leaking faucet, a malfunctioning electrical outlet, or a worn-out roof can catch you off guard.

Having an emergency fund for unforeseen repairs provides financial security and peace of mind.

6. Personalizing Your Space

Your home is a canvas for personal expression. Embark on the journey of making it uniquely yours by decorating, painting, and adding your personal touch. This process doesn't need to happen overnight; take the time to curate a space that reflects your personality and style.

7. Embracing The Transition

Transitioning into a new home is not just about adjusting to a physical space; it's also about embracing change. While nostalgia for your previous residence is natural, focusing on the positive aspects of your new home and the memories you'll create here helps in fully embracing this new chapter of your life.

As we draw the curtains on this exploration of post-home purchase life, one thing becomes abundantly clear: owning a home is not just a transaction; it's a transformation. The journey of homeownership extends far beyond the dotted line on the contract—it's a journey that unfolds with every day you spend in your new abode.

Embracing the post-purchase period involves more than just navigating practicalities; it's about embracing change, forging connections, and creating memories. Your new home becomes a backdrop for the moments that shape your life—birthdays celebrated, quiet evenings enjoyed, and the laughter of loved ones echoing through its halls.

Remember that the transition takes time. As you settle into your new environment, allow yourself the space to adjust, familiarize yourself with your neighborhood, and develop a sense of belonging. Establishing routines and connections will gradually transform your house into a home.

Budgeting for ongoing expenses and unexpected repairs ensures that your investment remains secure. Regular maintenance not only preserves the value of your property but also creates an environment where you can thrive.

Personalizing your space is an act of self-expression—a canvas on which you paint your unique story. The process might take time, but the result is a sanctuary that resonates with your personality and style.

The post-home purchase journey is an opportunity to embrace change and growth. As you navigate the path ahead, keep in mind that each experience, whether anticipated or unexpected, contributes to the rich tapestry of your life.

Owning a home is a privilege—a testament to your hard work and aspirations. As you walk through the rooms, envision the memories you'll create, the milestones you'll achieve, and the legacy you'll leave behind. Your home is more than just bricks and mortar; it's a reflection of who you are and the life you're building.

In this concluding chapter of our guide, we encourage you to approach this new phase with open arms and an open heart. Embrace the journey, celebrate the milestones, and cherish every moment. From settling into personalizing your space, from budgeting to navigating new dynamics, each step is a building block in the grand narrative of homeownership. So go forth, ready to live, learn, and make the most of every adventure your new home brings.

CHAPTER 18.

HOMEOWNERSHIP OR RENTING: MAKING THE RIGHT CHOICE FOR YOU

The age-old question of whether to buy a home or continue renting is a fundamental crossroad that has the power to shape your financial landscape and lifestyle aspirations. It's a decision that transcends mere housing options; it's a choice that influences your long-term financial security, personal goals, and sense of stability. As you stand at this intersection, the path to homeownership might seem paved with dreams of equity and nesting, while the route of renting offers the allure of flexibility and reduced responsibilities.

In this comprehensive guide, we delve into the intricate world of homeownership versus renting, illuminating the pros and cons of each choice. While there's no universal answer that fits every individual, understanding the nuances of both options will empower you to make a decision that aligns with your unique circumstances and aspirations.

This exploration goes beyond the mere comparison of finances; it's a journey into understanding the true implications of each choice. It's about more than calculating mortgage rates and rent costs—it's about envisioning the life you want to lead and the financial roadmap that supports your vision. By diving into the intricacies of both homeownership and renting, you're equipping yourself with the knowledge needed to make an informed decision—one that's grounded in both practicality and personal fulfilment.

So, whether you're a first-time homebuyer ready to embark on a new chapter or someone reevaluating your living situation, this guide is designed to help you navigate the complexities of this pivotal decision. Let's explore the benefits and considerations of both paths, unravelling the layers of financial commitment, lifestyle choices, and long-term prospects. By the time you've reached the end of this journey, you'll be armed with the insights needed to confidently answer the question: Should you buy a home or continue to rent?

The Case For Homeownership

1. Building Equity:

Perhaps one of the most compelling reasons to consider homeownership is the opportunity to build equity. With every mortgage payment, you're effectively paying off a portion of your loan and increasing your ownership stake in the property. Over time, this can result in significant financial gain as your property appreciates in value. It's like putting money into a long-term investment that you can eventually leverage for other financial goals.

2. Stability And Personalization:

Owning a home provides a sense of stability that's hard to replicate while renting. You have the freedom to create a space that truly reflects your personality, and you're not subject to the whims of a landlord's rules. This aspect can be particularly appealing for families or individuals who desire a sense of permanence and a place to truly call their own.

3. Investment Potential:

Real estate has historically been a reliable investment avenue. While property values can experience fluctuations, the long-term trajectory tends to be upward. Investing in a home can potentially offer financial rewards when it comes time to sell. It's a tangible asset that can diversify your investment portfolio.

4. Tax Benefits:

Homeownership often comes with tax advantages that can positively impact your overall financial picture. Mortgage interest and property tax deductions can reduce your taxable income, putting more money back into your pocket. This financial reprieve is not something that renters typically enjoy.

The Case For Renting

1. Flexibility:

Renting offers a level of flexibility that homeownership can't match. If your life circumstances change—a new job opportunity, a desire to explore a different neighborhood, or even the need to downsize—you can more easily make these adjustments without the complexities of selling a property. This flexibility can be a significant advantage, particularly for those with evolving life plans.

Lower Upfront Costs: While purchasing a home can require a substantial down payment, closing costs, and ongoing maintenance expenses, renting usually involves lower upfront costs. Typically, renters only need to provide a security deposit and possibly the first and last month's rent. This lower financial barrier can be more accessible, especially for those just starting their careers or saving for other financial goals.

2. Predictable Expenses:

Renting often comes with more predictable monthly expenses. While rent might increase over time, homeowners can face fluctuations in mortgage payments due to changes in interest rates or property taxes. For renters, the certainty of stable monthly costs can provide peace of mind for budgeting and planning.

3. No Maintenance Responsibility:

One of the significant perks of renting is the lack of maintenance responsibility. Landlords are typically responsible for repairs and maintenance tasks. This can save you both time and money compared to the ongoing upkeep required in homeownership.

Factors To Consider

1. Financial Readiness:

Assess your financial situation honestly. Do you have a stable income, a good credit score, and a sufficient down payment saved up? Owning a home requires financial stability, not just for the initial purchase but also for ongoing expenses and potential unexpected repairs.

2. Long-Term Plans:

Consider your long-term plans. How long do you intend to stay in the area? If you anticipate moving within a few years, renting might be a more practical choice, as the costs and complexities of buying and selling a property might not be justified.

3. Lifestyle Preferences:

Your lifestyle and life stage play a crucial role in this decision. Do you value the stability and ability to personalize your living space that homeownership offers? Or do you prioritize flexibility and the ability to easily relocate without the burden of property ownership?

4. Market Conditions:

Research the real estate market in your area. Are home prices on the rise? Are interest rates favorable? Understanding the current market conditions can significantly influence your decision. It's essential to buy in a market that aligns with your long-term goals.

5. Financial Goals:

Consider your broader financial goals. Do you want to allocate your funds towards homeownership, or would you prefer to invest them differently? It's crucial to ensure that your choice aligns with your financial trajectory.

Ultimately, the decision between buying a home and renting is a deeply personal one. Both options have their merits and drawbacks, and the right choice for you depends on a multitude of factors. Carefully assess your financial readiness, long-term plans, and lifestyle preferences. Remember that homeownership is a long-term commitment that requires thorough financial planning and the willingness to invest time and effort into maintaining your property. On the other hand, renting offers flexibility and fewer upfront costs, allowing you to explore different paths without being tied to a particular location.

By understanding the pros and cons of each option and considering your unique circumstances, you can make a decision that aligns with your goals and sets you on a path toward financial well-being and personal satisfaction. Whether you choose to embark on the journey of homeownership or opt for the flexibility of renting, this decision marks a pivotal step in your life's narrative. Make it wisely, armed with knowledge and a clear understanding of your priorities.

Trusted References for Understanding Homeownership vs. Renting: Expert Insights and Comprehensive Guidance

When it comes to making the decision between homeownership and renting, it's essential to gather information from reputable sources that offer a comprehensive understanding of both options. One of the most trusted and respected references in the realm of personal finance and real estate is the **U.S. Department of Housing and Urban Development (HUD)**. They provide a wealth of resources, including articles, guides, and tools, to help individuals navigate the decision-making process. Visit their website at www.hud.gov to access valuable information about homeownership and renting.

Additionally, the **National Association of Realtors (NAR)** offers valuable insights into the benefits of homeownership, market trends, and the economic impact of real estate. They provide research-backed information that can shed light on the advantages of owning a home. Explore their website at www.nar.realtor to access valuable data and expert analysis.

For a balanced perspective, consult financial platforms like **The Balance** (Visit their website at www.thebalance.com for a balanced perspective on this important decision) or **Investopedia**, (Explore their website at www.investopedia.com for comprehensive information) which often publish in-depth articles that weigh the pros and cons of homeownership versus renting. These platforms offer well-researched insights backed by financial experts.

The Balance: The Balance offers well-researched articles that weigh the pros and cons of homeownership versus renting. Visit their website at www.thebalance.com for a balanced perspective on this important decision.

Moreover, for a more localized approach, consider checking out **local real estate agencies** or **property management companies** that can provide insights into the current market conditions and rental options in your area. Remember that a well-rounded understanding of this topic requires gathering information from multiple reputable sources, as it involves intricate financial considerations, lifestyle preferences, and long-term goals. By exploring these trusted references, you can make an informed decision that aligns with your unique circumstances and aspirations.

ABOUT THE AUTHOR

Randika Attanayaka (Roo)

Randika (Roo) is a captivating fusion of an author, marketing specialist, mindfulness researcher, yoga devotee, eco-traveler, and an engaging blogger. This concise Kindle biography unveils the remarkable journey of an individual whose diverse passions merge into a narrative of love, connection, and purpose.

Known for crafting tales of love and passion, Randika (Roo) paints vivid emotional landscapes through his writing, resonating deeply with readers seeking heartfelt narratives.

In the marketing sphere, his expertise in understanding human behavior and innovative strategies mirrors the depth of insights found within his storytelling.

Parallel to his career, Randika (Roo) delves into mindfulness research and the transformative impact of yoga, seeking inner peace and balance in his personal life.

BOOKS BY THIS AUTHOR

Tickle Talk 101: "Mastering The Art Of Handling Your Playful Woman With Humor And Love"

Start your journey to a life filled with laughter, love and fun with "Mastering the Art of Handling Your Playful Woman with Humor and Love"! In this witty and insightful book, you'll learn the secrets to handling the spirited woman of your dreams with wit, charm and a dash of mischievousness. With this trusty guide, you'll discover how to decode her cryptic texts, navigate the rollercoaster of her emotions, and turn everyday moments into uproarious adventures.

Don't miss out on this uproariously funny, yet profoundly heartwarming guide to building a connection that's as strong as it is playful. Buy now before the price changes!